17 *Memphis Belle* B-17 crew are celebrated as first Flying Fortress to survive twenty-five bombing missions over German-occupied Europe.

30 Josef Mengele becomes "camp doctor" at Auschwitz-Birkenau. Performs cruel experiments on children, twins, dwarfs; supervises gas chambers.

JUNE

Manhattan Project. Scientists at Los Alamos laboratories in New Mexico begin work on atomic bomb.

2 First combat mission for "Tuskegee Airmen," only African-American fighter pilots to serve in U.S. Army Air Force during war.

10 U.S. Eighth Air Force begins Operation Pointblank, code name for massive bombing offensive against Germany. Highest priority is to destroy Luftwaffe (German Air Force) and secure way for Allied ground invasion of Europe.

JULY

9 Allies invade Sicily.

25 Italians overthrow and arrest Fascist dictator Benito Mussolini.

AUGUST

5 WASPs (Women's Airforce Service Pilots) created for one thousand American women who test-piloted, trained gunners, and delivered planes in the United States.

17 Daylight bombing strategy questioned after United States suffers huge casualties in raid on Schweinfurt-Regensburg (Germany).

SEPTEMBER

3 Allies invade Italian mainland; Italy secretly surrenders.

9 Allies land at Salerno and Taranto in Italy.

OCTOBER

13 New Italian government joins Allies; declares war on Germany.

14 Second American bombing raid on Schweinfurt-Regensburg results in unacceptably high loss of bombers; causes temporary halt to bombing over central Germany.

NOVEMBER

26 World's first jet fighter plane demonstrated for Hitler; deployment delayed by his order to have it redesigned as bomber.

28 (- December 1) Teheran Conference. Soviet leader Joseph Stalin meets with Winston Churchill and Franklin D. Roosevelt to plan European invasion.

DECEMBER

24 General Dwight D. Eisenhower named Supreme Commander of Allied Expeditionary Force to direct invasion of [...]

[...] Anzio, [...] [...]ern Italy.

27 After nine hundred days, Siege of Leningrad ends with German defeat.

FEBRUARY

20-25 "Big Week" for U.S. Eighth Air Force. Bombers, escorted by new long-range P-51 fighters, resume missions over central Germany.

MARCH

4 U.S. Eighth Air Force begins first daylight attacks on Berlin.

31 Allied air superiority over Europe achieved; Allies begin losing more bombers to antiaircraft fire than to German fighter planes.

JUNE

4 Rome is first Axis capital city to fall to Allies. Civilians welcome American troops with kisses and cheers.

THE BELLY GUNNER

THE BELLY GUNNER

CAROL EDGEMON HIPPERSON

TWENTY-FIRST CENTURY BOOKS   BROOKFIELD, CONNECTICUT

DEDICATION

To the American veterans of World War II: Thank you for your service and your sacrifice.

ACKNOWLEDGMENTS

Thanks to my husband, Brian G. Hipperson, who not only tolerated my need for time to work, but also supported, advised, and encouraged me from start to finish.

Thanks also to these friends and relatives who gave assistance and advice at crucial junctures: Janie Aldrich Hickel, Lila Aldrich, Roy and Louise Hipperson, John and Jean Newby, Dave and Kathy Dormaier, Charles Edgemon, Allen Jorgensen, Alexandra and Meredith Hipperson, Sly Chatman, Nick Thiry, Ron Gies, Willem and Eppe Bosch, Kathy Kinsella Ybarra, Kate Carey, and Bob Brunkow.

A number of students at Spokane's Central Valley High School helped with the historical research, including Tim Broderius, Jeff Kempff, Chris Reilly, Erin MacGregor, and, especially, Nick Hopper. At Bowdish Junior High School, also in Spokane, the seventh- and eighth-grade language arts classes were a wonderfully curious and attentive first audience; their questions led to important improvements in the first draft. Thank you to their teachers, Bill Bussard and Cheryl Welch, and their librarian, Susan Fox, for letting me visit their classrooms.

I am particularly grateful to James H. Keeffe Jr., Lt. Colonel, USAF (retired), for his careful reading and suggestions for improving the manuscript's historical accuracy. For their help in acquiring more photographs than I ever thought possible, many thanks to the following: Larry and Irene Weir; Dave Purtill; Pete Anest; Walter Jefferson of the NPRC (National Personnel Records Center); Director Frederick D. Brown and M/Sgt. Gary McNeese at Fairchild Heritage Museum; Bill Morton, Bill Nagle, Geoffrey Blank, and Andy Bredeson at the Confederate Air Force (Arizona Wing) Museum.

Above all others, I thank Dale Wilfred Aldrich and the angel who convinced him to remember a great deal more than he thought he could, or should.

Published by Twenty-First Century Books
A Division of The Millbrook Press, Inc.
2 Old New Milford Road, Brookfield, CT 06804
www.millbrookpress.com

Library of Congress Cataloging-in-Publication Data
Aldrich, Dale.
The belly gunner / [compiled] by Carol Edgemon Hipperson.
p. cm.
An interview with Dale Aldrich.
Includes bibliographical references and index.
ISBN 0-7613-1873-9 (lib. bdg.)
1. Aldrich, Dale. 2. World War, 1939–1945—Personal narratives, American. 3. United States. Army Air Forces—Non-commissioned officers—Biography. 4. Flight crews—United States—Biography. 5. World War, 1939–1945—Aerial operations, American. 6. World War, 1939–1945—Prisoners and prisons, Germany. 7. World War, 1939–1945—Campaigns—Germany. 8. Stalag XVII B Krems-Gneixendorf. [1. Aldrich, Dale. 2. World War, 1939–1945—Personal narratives, American. 3. World War, 1939–1945—Aerial operations, American. 4. Prisoners of war. 5. Stalag XVII B Krems-Gneixendorf.]
I. Hipperson, Carol Edgemon. II. Title.
D790 .A782 2001
940.54'4973'092—dc21   00-047933

CONTENTS

Preface 7

Introduction 9

1. **DRAFTED** *11*

2. **AIR COLLEGE** *16*

3. **FROM MECHANIC TO GUNNER** *22*

4. **THE FLYING FORTRESS** *28*

5. **CROSSING THE ATLANTIC** *42*

6. **HORHAM AIR BASE** *46*

7. **THE MÜNSTER MISSION** *57*

8. **SHOT DOWN** *64*

9. **BAILING OUT** *68*

10. **BETRAYED AND CAPTURED** *71*

11. **PRISONER OF WAR** *74*

12. **INTERROGATION BY THE NAZIS** *79*

13. **STALAG 17** *84*

14. **447 DAYS** *89*

15. **UNUSUAL INCIDENTS AT STALAG 17** *104*

16. **THE MARCH TO GERMANY** *115*

17. **LIBERATION** *122*

18. **CAMP LUCKY STRIKE** *126*

19. **HOMECOMING** *131*

Epilogue 139

Glossary 149

For Further Reading 152

Index 156

ABOUT THE SIDE NOTES AND TIMELINE

Most of Dale Aldrich's story is self-explanatory. But some of the people, places, terms, and events may be unfamiliar. In addition, readers may want to put the dates mentioned in the story into the historical context of World War II and the Holocaust.

For this reason the author has created several aids for reference. Side notes keyed by number to the narrative explain some terms, names, places, and events. Others are defined in the glossary near the end of the book. Additional notes, called "Coinciding Dates," identify events that were taking place elsewhere in the world at the time the belly gunner's story unfolds. Timelines at the front and back of the book provide a chronology of important World War II and Holocaust events.

PREFACE

In April 1995 I received a call from my friend Janie Aldrich Hickel, a medical missionary in Africa. She knew her father had been a gunner on a B-17 bomber during World War II because he'd told her parts of the story when she was a child. Now she wanted to know the rest of his story and asked for my help in obtaining it so that others could enjoy it, too. I willingly agreed.

Janie's father, Dale Aldrich, was seventy-four in 1995 when I began the first of what turned out to be a series of ten three-hour interviews. We'd meet when he came to Spokane for one of his American Ex-Prisoner of War gatherings, usually at his hotel—sometimes in the lobby, sometimes over dinner in the restaurant or cocktail lounge. Dale usually came alone to the interviews; occasionally his wife, Lila, would join us.

Dale would talk, and I'd ask questions and take notes. The interviews lasted until he felt tired or until I got a headache from concentrating so hard.

At first, Dale was very reluctant. Like so many of the rapidly diminishing number of American veterans who fought in World War II, he didn't think he had done anything special. He couldn't believe he could remember enough to be of much interest. If his daughter had not begged him to submit to the interviews, he would not have cooperated at all.

As it turned out, Dale Aldrich remembered a great deal. His is a remarkable story of how one small-town American GI experienced a terrible war. It is a story of patriotism and service, love and friendship, perseverance and endurance—all the stuff heroes are made of—told in a way that makes clear to all why the entire world owes so much to the American veterans of World War II.

Carol Edgemon Hipperson
Spokane, Washington

Flames rise into a black sky following the Japanese surprise attack on Pearl Harbor, December 7, 1941—an attack that killed or wounded 3,432 American soldiers and 103 civilians.

INTRODUCTION

The belly gunner's story begins late in 1941, right after the Japanese attacked Pearl Harbor in the Hawaiian Islands, the main base for the United States' Pacific Fleet. By then, most of Europe and much of North Africa and Asia had been at war for some time.

World War II had begun, as most wars do, with an outbreak of violence between two countries. In Europe, it started in 1939, when Adolf Hitler ordered German forces into Poland. From there the powerful German army and air force continued to advance. By late 1941, Great Britain and the Soviet Union were the only European countries openly defending themselves from German occupation. Americans were concerned and sympathetic, but most did not wish to become involved in what appeared to be just another European conflict over national boundaries.

In Asia, the war started in 1931, when Japan invaded the Chinese territory of Manchuria. By late 1941, the United States was the only country with a navy powerful enough to oppose Japanese plans to conquer the rest of Asia, Australia, and all the islands in the western Pacific.

Headlines announce the attack on Pearl Harbor.

DRAFTED

I wasn't really *for* the war until Pearl Harbor.[1] After that, everybody I knew was going into some branch of the military, and I wanted to go, too. My mother was afraid I was going to enlist; she made me swear I wouldn't. She'd lost two sons to illness already—I was the only boy left in the family—and she didn't want to lose me. Mom just wanted me to stay home and go back to college in the fall.

I kept my promise to my mother. I didn't volunteer, that is, but it was mainly because I knew it didn't matter. I'd turned twenty-one in February, which was just a couple of months after the start of the war. I wasn't going to college at the time and I was single, so I figured I'd get drafted.[2]

Sure enough, I got my draft notice in July. It was in a letter that started out, "Your friends and neighbors have chosen you . . . ." I thought that was pretty funny. I wish I'd kept that letter, but I didn't.

[1] The United States was still officially neutral on December 7, 1941, when Japanese planes bombed the U.S. naval base in Pearl Harbor. The United States declared war on Japan on December 8. Because Germany and Italy were allies of Japan, both declared war on the United States on December 11. This led to full U.S. engagement in World War II as one of the Allies.

[2] During World War II, all American men between the ages of eighteen and sixty-five registered for the draft, although no one over thirty-six was actually called. By the end of 1942, the United States was drafting 500,000 men per month.

3 Of the approximately 50 million American men who registered with the Selective Service, about 35 million were deferred due to the nature of their work, the number of their dependents, or their age.

4 NAZI is an acronym from four letters of the *Nationalsozialistische Deutsche Arbeiters Partei*, or National Socialist German Workers' Party. The Nazi party, represented by a black swastika on a red flag, was in power throughout the war. Adolf Hitler joined the party shortly after it was founded in Munich in 1919 and was elected "unlimited chairman" two years later.

5 More than five million draft registrants were rejected because of physical, mental, or educational deficiencies.

I was driving tractor for a farmer in Coulee City [small town in eastern Washington] that summer. He told me he could probably get me deferred.[3] I don't know how he thought he could do that, unless it was because he was a farmer. I knew farmers usually got draft deferments, but I didn't know if that applied to their employees, too. Maybe I could have gotten out of it, but I told him no.

I thought it was pretty hopeless to try for a deferment. Besides, I really wanted to go. I knew it wasn't safe, but I wasn't afraid. I was young and single, still living at home with my parents. There was nothing else I really wanted to do right then. I guess I was like everybody else who was going into the service in those days. Sure, I loved my country. And we were all really mad at the Japanese after Pearl Harbor. We were mad at the Germans, too. We figured if we didn't fight the Nazis[4] over there in Europe, sooner or later we'd have to fight them here, maybe even in Washington and Oregon. And I suppose I thought I would be missing out on some big adventure if I didn't go to war.

My draft notice said for me to report to Fort Lewis in Tacoma [Washington] on the second of August. That was the nearest army induction center at that time. I caught the bus from Coulee City to Ephrata, and from there to Tacoma. There were fourteen guys altogether in my group, all from the Grand Coulee area. I only knew one of them, a kid from Wilson Creek named Bob Biggs.

When we got to Tacoma, the Army put us up in the basement of this old hotel. We took our physicals the very next day. I remember there was this one guy from Hartline. He was happy because he had a hernia and failed the physical.[5] I was glad I passed. I would have been real unhappy if I hadn't. I wanted to go.

After our physicals, we got our serial numbers assigned to us. Mine was 39184867. That went on my dog tag. A dog tag is this little piece of metal shaped in a rectangle. You had your name engraved on it, your religion, and your next of kin—whoever you wanted notified in case you were killed or injured. Mine had a "P" for Protestant and my dad's name and address.

Everybody got two dog tags with the same information engraved on each, and you had to wear them both around your neck on this chain made out of little steel balls. You weren't ever supposed to take them off, not even to shower. We had to have two dog tags because, if you got killed, the grave people would stick one of the tags in your mouth. That's why each tag had a notch cut out of it, so it could be wedged between a guy's teeth after he was dead. The second tag was for the grave people to take back to headquarters, for record keeping, I guess.[6]

We were told the Air Force needed two hundred men immediately, so I was selected for that. I didn't have any choice. They could have put me in the regular Army or the Navy instead, but right then the greatest need was for the Air Force. They didn't tell us why.[7] Actually, it wasn't even called the Air Force then; it was the Army Air Corps. At that time the Air Force was not a separate branch of the military like it is now; it was just another subdivision of the Army.

If I'd had a choice, I would have liked to have gone into the paratroopers. To me that sounded kind of exciting, to get to fly around the world and jump out of airplanes. But the Air Force needed me someplace else. I probably wouldn't have qualified for the paratroopers anyway. Those guys had to carry a lot of gear, and

Dale Aldrich's dog tag

[6] The U.S. Air Force still issues two metal identification tags to to be worn around the neck, but, in a custom that evolved during the war in Vietnam, one of these is often intertwined with the laces inside the airman's boot. And, although one dog tag is still placed in the mouth for identification of the dead, final and official identification can now be performed by DNA analysis.

[7] Airmen were needed for aerial bombing, a key element of the Allies' plan to defeat Germany. Although the first American bombers arrived in England in July 1942, the bombing plan could not be fully implemented until many more planes, flight crews, and aircraft mechanics could be transported to air bases in England.

Pvt. Dale Aldrich wearing his Class-A uniform while at Basic Training at Fort Lewis, Tacoma, Washington, August 1942.

1942

I was only five foot six and about 140 pounds. I'm sure the Army would have said I wasn't big enough.

I got sworn in on August 4. There were only eight or ten of us in my group by then. We were still in our civilian clothes when they took us to a hotel room, up the stairs in that same hotel where we'd been staying in the basement. There were a few officers in the room when they let us in. One of them—I think he was a sergeant—told us to raise our right hands, and then he said something about upholding the laws of the United States of America. It was just a couple of sentences; the whole thing was pretty informal. After that, the Army sent us back to Ephrata by bus. We all got two weeks at home to settle our affairs before we were supposed to report back to Fort Lewis.

I didn't have too much to do when I got back to Coulee City, except I did have to say good-bye to my girlfriend. We'd been going together since high school. We talked about getting married, but we decided to put it off and see how we felt after the war. She said she would wait for me. I didn't believe her. I just had a hunch. It was just a high-school kind of thing we had. Still, if I hadn't been drafted, I wouldn't be surprised if I'd have ended up married to her.

My orders were to report back to Fort Lewis on August 16 for Basic Training. That time, instead of taking the bus, I got to take the train from Ephrata to Tacoma.

There was nothing fun about Basic. That old drill sergeant just marched the heck out of us, and if you didn't start out on your left foot you were in trouble. Some guys couldn't get it—couldn't remember which was their left and which was their right. The drill sergeant finally made one guy carry a brick in his left hand whenever we marched. That was supposed to teach him which foot to start with.

The worst part about Basic Training was they made me take every vaccination there was, and all of them made me sick. Especially the typhoid shot. That one gave me a real bad fever, and it was a really hot August in Tacoma in 1942. Between the heat and the humidity and the fever from the typhoid shot, I thought I was going to die.

About the time I got to feeling better, I was told I was part of a group that was being sent to finish Basic Training at Jefferson Barracks, Missouri. That was another Army Air Corps base outside of St. Louis.[8] We traveled by troop train, and it seemed like I barely got off the train when they started giving me boosters for all those shots I'd had back in Tacoma. Of course, those made me sick, too.

Basic Training got over in September. I thought I might get to go home for a while, but I wasn't that lucky. I got sent right away to East St. Louis, Illinois, instead. The Army said I'd been picked for something called "Air College."

8 Jefferson Barracks, St. Louis, Missouri, was the first of seven centers the Army created from 1940 to 1943 to train new Air Corps recruits.

AIR COLLEGE

Air College was for training aircraft mechanics. I didn't ask to be any kind of mechanic, but one of the first questions the Army asked me when I got drafted was, "What line of work are you in?" Well, of course I answered I'd been driving tractor on a farm, so they probably assumed I already had some experience at repairing heavy equipment.

It turned out I was one of two hundred who had been selected back at Fort Lewis for Air College.[1] I remember when they told us, they said we were the cream of the crop. And then some guy way in the back said, "Yeah, but the cream went sour." He was just being silly, but we all knew damn good and well we weren't that special. We just happened to be there when they needed two hundred guys in the Air Force.

I do know at that point in the war, in late 1942, the Air Corps really needed aircraft mechanics. It sure wasn't what I had in mind

Parks Air College, East St. Louis, Illinois, was one of the original seven civilian schools the Army contracted in 1939 for training Air Corps mechanics.

for myself for a career, but Air College was pretty good duty. The only thing I didn't like about it was we had to sleep during the day and then get up and go to school at night. There in East St. Louis they were training both civilian and military aircraft mechanics. The civilians got to go to school during the day; the military got the same classes at night. I think we even had some of the same instructors as the civilians.

Our classroom was this big shop. There were a few lectures on aerodynamics, but they didn't give us any textbooks or tests or anything like that. Mostly the instructors just taught us how to handle different kinds of tools. A lot of the guys had never even seen a hacksaw before; they didn't know diddly. The classes were all pretty easy for me, because my dad was in the car business, and I'd been helping around the garage since I was a kid. Mechanically, airplanes are not that much different from cars.

I did learn how to use some special tools, though, and they showed us how the wings on most small airplanes were actually made of wood with fabric stretched over it. Why they bothered to teach us that, I don't know. The wings on most of the Army's planes were being made out of aluminum. Maybe the instructors were still used to working on the older planes, the ones they used to have in the old Army Signal Corps.

There were about 150 of us going to Air College, and we all had to live together in this old shoe factory. The factory wasn't operating at the time. In fact, it looked like it had been out of business for a long while. Whoever it was that owned the factory had a contract with the Army to house and feed us.

The shoe factory had this one big empty room with nothing in it but bunk beds. That was our barracks. Down in the basement there was a cafeteria set up for our meals, and the food they served was pretty good, too. Every night after dinner the Army had buses ready to take us from East St. Louis to our classes in St. Louis over on the Missouri side of the Mississippi River. It was only about a half-hour bus trip each way.

I was a buck private then, so my pay was fifty dollars a month. I also got to keep whatever money was left over from what the Army was paying the factory owner for my meals. Altogether, I was making around a hundred dollars a month. That was a pretty good deal, quite a bit of money for a single guy in those days. I spent most of it on entertainment. There was a USO club across the river, so we'd all go over there on weekends. The Army didn't provide any buses for us to get there, so we usually took taxis. That was a fairly expensive way to get around, but beer was only fifteen cents a glass.

USO is for United Service Organizations.[2] Anybody in uniform was welcome at a USO club. The one in St. Louis was really big, a masonry building that covered a whole city block. It could hold thousands of people, and it was always crowded whenever I was there. You'd see guys from every branch of the service, and lots of girls. The girls were USO volunteers. You could ask any one of them to dance with you, and none of them would ever turn you down.

There was always a live band that played "big band" or "swing" music for dancing. I remember Glenn Miller's band played one

⭐ **2** During the war the USO operated three thousand clubs throughout the United States for entertaining soldiers.

At the typical USO, GIs came to relax, socialize, dance, and meet girls.

night. That was really good music. Another time we had the Tommy Dorsey band. Jimmy Dorsey's, too. All those bands just traveled around during the war, playing for servicemen at the USO clubs all over the country.

The USO in St. Louis had windows and plenty of lights on all the time. It did have a bar where you could buy beer and soft drinks, and there were lots of tables if you wanted to sit down and talk or eat instead of dancing. They didn't serve hard liquor and the food was just sandwiches and snacks, but you didn't have to pay for any of it. Everything except your beverages was free.

One night—I think it was in late October or early November—I met this girl named Jackie at the USO. She was real pretty, kind of tall for a girl—about the same height as me—and she had this really long brown hair. She was a good dancer, too, which was probably what attracted me to her in the first place, and she liked to laugh and have a good time.

Jackie lived with her mother in St. Louis. She could speak pretty good French because her mother had been a French war bride from World War I. I never met her father. He was in some kind of a hospital the whole time I was there. I think it must have been a mental institution. Jackie said it was because he'd been gassed.[3]

Jackie was a secretary for her regular job, but she also did volunteer work for the Red Cross. She and her mother both helped pack the Red Cross parcels that were going out from the States to prisoners of war all over the world.[4]

I was getting letters from my girlfriend back home, about one a week, and she sent me a real nice picture of herself. I kept that in

[3] The Germans were the first to gas enemy forces—use chemical weapons against them—during World War I (1914–1918).

[4] During World War II American Red Cross volunteers packed and shipped approximately 27 million parcels of food and supplies to American and Allied prisoners of war.

my wallet. Still, I would have been a lot lonelier there in St. Louis if it hadn't been for Jackie. At Christmas, she and her mom even invited me to their house for dinner. Her two aunts from Iowa were there, too, and I brought another guy—a friend of mine from Air College by the name of Buckmaster. That day and evening there at Jackie's house with her family was my first Christmas away from home. I didn't really notice how homesick I was until then. And when I heard "White Christmas"[5] on the radio for the first time that night, well, that just made it worse.

I did like Jackie a lot, though, and we spent as much time together as we could while I was going to Air College. I remember one time she was with me when I took out my wallet and she saw the picture of my girlfriend back home. She asked me, "Who's that girl?" I said it was my sister Patsy. I don't think she bought it, though. She just laughed and said, "Oh, *sure* it is." To me, Jackie and I were just really good friends, not lovers. I wasn't there long enough to get into that kind of a relationship with her.[6]

I graduated from Air College on New Year's Eve, 1942. I didn't know enough people in St. Louis to have a party, but I didn't feel like celebrating much, anyway. That night Jackie and I just went over to the USO. She said she would write to me. I believed she would.

★5 A popular Christmas song written by Irving Berlin in 1942 and first recorded by Bing Crosby.

★6 Time to complete a basic airplane mechanics course at a civilian contract school such as Parks Air College in 1942 was 112 days.

1942

COINCIDING DATES
WHILE ALDRICH ATTENDED AIR COLLEGE, SEPTEMBER TO DECEMBER 1942, THE ALLIES INVADED NORTH AFRICA AND
DEFEATED JAPANESE FORCES AT GUADALCANAL IN THE PACIFIC. (SEE TIMELINE.)

FROM MECHANIC TO GUNNER

The day after I graduated from Air College I got transferred to the air base at San Antonio, Texas, for duty as an aircraft mechanic. In the unit I was assigned to, there were about a hundred of us. The Army didn't have enough barracks to house everyone on the base, so my unit had to live in tents.

There were six guys to a tent, and every tent had a natural-gas stove with an upside-down funnel on top. Sometimes, just for fun, the guys would turn on the gas and let it build up a while. Then they'd throw a match at the stove and there would be this big explosion. It was a pretty dumb thing to do, but I never heard of anybody getting hurt or starting a fire that way. We were basically a bunch of kids. Pranks like that went on all the time. Maybe it was a way of coping with the stress of being away from home and with the uncertainty. For me that was it—the uncertainty—the not knowing when or if you were going to be sent somewhere else because of the war.

I had to work the graveyard shift.[1] I didn't mind that so much, except we didn't get anything to eat during the whole night because the mess hall was closed from dinnertime to breakfast. All we got was whatever was in the vending machines. I heard that the cooks used to send sandwiches over for the graveyard shift workers, but they had to quit doing that because we didn't have any refrigerators. One time the sandwiches spoiled, and some guys got sick.

After we got off work at seven in the morning, we had to walk two miles back to our tents. Then we'd go to the mess hall for breakfast, but the cooks were always mad at us for wanting to eat at 7 A.M. That was two hours later than when they served breakfast to everybody else, so the cooks were busy cleaning up about the time we came in to eat. They sure didn't like it when they had to stop and feed us, and sometimes there wasn't much food left.

I usually went to bed right after breakfast, but then I had to get up in a couple of hours or I'd miss lunch. You couldn't go back to bed after lunch until daily inspection, and then, if you didn't get up again in a couple of hours, you missed dinner. It just seemed like I never could get enough to eat.

I hadn't been working that schedule for very many days when I heard somebody say the Air Corps needed gunners.[2] I went right over and told our company clerk I wanted to sign up for gunners' school. "Gunner!" he said. "Why, that's dangerous! You could get killed being a gunner!" And I said, "Yeah, but if I stay here any longer, I'm gonna *starve* to death."

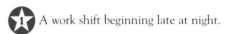 A work shift beginning late at night.

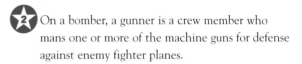 On a bomber, a gunner is a crew member who mans one or more of the machine guns for defense against enemy fighter planes.

At that point in my life, I didn't really know what I was cut out for. I got mostly C's in high school, but Coulee City High School didn't teach you much. They did offer French, which the principal said I needed for college, so I took that. I got an A in algebra at college. I don't know where I would have ended up if it hadn't been for the war. Some kind of business, probably, since that was what I was majoring in.

I knew for sure if I stayed an aircraft mechanic I'd be doomed to a real dull dead-end job. I think I might have seen gunnery school as a chance to find a little more excitement. Since the Air Force said they needed gunners, then I'd be a gunner. Patriotism was part of it, but mainly I just wanted to get out of San Antonio and *do* something.

After I applied for gunnery school, I had to take another physical. I think that must have been in April. Well, of course I'd worked all night the night before so my eyes were really tired, and I couldn't pass the eye-test part. The doctor told me I could come back the next day and retake the eye test if I really wanted to. I did, and that time I passed it.

A few nights after that, three or four of us decided to go to a Grange Hall dance we'd heard about in Fredericksburg [town outside San Antonio]. Generally, the guys I picked to hang out with were ones that liked to laugh a lot. We didn't drink that much beer, but we liked to have a good time. We especially liked to go to dances and meet girls. It was hard to meet girls at the dances in San Antonio because of the air base. There must have been about ten

GIs[3] for every girl, and you couldn't even get near the really good-looking ones. So, to get away from the competition, my buddies and I went to dances in the smaller towns whenever we could.

Fredericksburg was at least fifty miles north of San Antonio. That was a little too far for us to take a taxi, so we hitchhiked. People would pick you up pretty good in those days, especially soldiers in uniform. Everybody knew the soldiers were protecting them, so I guess they were glad to pay us back for serving the country. I think we made the trip in only about an hour or so.

After the dance we all went together and shared one motel room, and then we hitchhiked back to San Antonio the next day. It took us a little longer than we expected; we didn't get to the base until almost noon. That was later than we were supposed to be, so I was pretty nervous when I heard the company clerk had been looking for me that morning. Somebody told me he was carrying some papers for me; I figured that meant I'd been caught AWOL.[4] I was really nervous by the time he found me. This was the same guy I'd talked to when I first applied to be a gunner. He sure had a lot of fun with me, teasing me about being AWOL, how I was probably going to get court-martialed and all. But when he finally gave me the papers, I saw they were my orders to report to gunnery school.

By May I was in Laredo, Texas, learning how to operate .50-caliber machine guns. Gunnery school was a five-week course. There were only about twenty-five guys in my class because the Army Air Corps' gunnery school was strictly for volunteers.[5] I didn't know

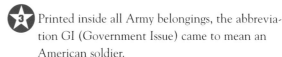 Printed inside all Army belongings, the abbreviation GI (Government Issue) came to mean an American soldier.

AWOL is an acronym for absent, or absence, without leave (permission), a serious infraction of military law and punishable by court-martial (military trial).

As the need for aerial gunners grew and casualties increased, the volunteer program ended and men were assigned to the position.

To supplement the pictures and silhouettes used for Army and Navy aircraft recognition training, the American government asked schoolchildren to make half a million model airplanes.

 In 1943 gunnery school graduates who had special technical training were immediately promoted to sergeant. Others remained privates until completion of a technical training course.

 The Geneva Convention Relative to the Treatment of Prisoners (1929), commonly referred to as the Geneva Convention, is an international agreement aimed at protecting the rights of prisoners of war and assuring humane treatment.

why at first. It wasn't until after I got into the course that I started to realize how dangerous it was.

We met in a classroom to study the silhouettes of fighter planes. There weren't any tests; you just had to study those pictures so you could identify all the different kinds of fighter planes you might see in air-to-air combat.[6] You really had to know how to tell "ours"—the P-38s and the P-47s—from "theirs"—the German Messerschmitts and the Junkers. We had to learn what the Zeros looked like, too. Those were the Japanese fighter planes. We had to recognize all of them because at that point nobody knew where we were going to end up. If they sent us to Europe, we'd be up against the Germans; if you got sent to the Pacific, you'd see combat with the Japanese.

When the course was over, I got promoted to sergeant. You had to be at least a sergeant to fly in combat.[7] That was because of the Geneva Convention[8] rules regarding prisoners of war. Officers, from sergeant on up, could not be made to work if captured. If your rank was less than a sergeant, your captors could make a slave out of you if they wanted to. Anybody who got orders to fly made sergeant's rank immediately because of that rule. There were four ranks of sergeant: buck, staff, technical, and master. I was a buck sergeant. I was scheduled for promotion to staff sergeant in six months, but, as it turned out, I didn't get that rank until about two years later.

My whole class got sent to Salt Lake City, Utah, after we graduated from gunnery school in June. That was where we were supposed to wait while the Air Corps decided where they were going to send us next.

I didn't worry about where I was going, didn't even think about it. Maybe I was getting used to the uncertainty by then. I was just looking forward to having a little time off to relax and see the sights in Salt Lake City. Instead, I came down with a really bad case of the flu and landed in the hospital for about a week. Right after that, I got my orders to go to Moses Lake [small town in Washington] of all places. Holy cow! Moses Lake was only about an hour's drive from my hometown.

COINCIDING DATES
IN THE FIRST HALF OF 1943, WHILE ALDRICH SERVED AS AN AIRCRAFT MECHANIC AND WENT TO GUNNERY SCHOOL, THE GERMANS SURRENDERED IN NORTH AFRICA AND THE USSR; THE ALLIES SET A HIGH PRIORITY ON ACHIEVING SUPERIORITY OVER THE LUFTWAFFE (GERMAN AIR FORCE). (SEE TIMELINE.)

1943

THE FLYING FORTRESS

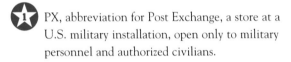

1. PX, abbreviation for Post Exchange, a store at a U.S. military installation, open only to military personnel and authorized civilians.

2. The B-17, a high-altitude bomber dubbed the Flying Fortress, was the first all metal four-engine monoplane bomber developed by the Boeing Airplane Company of Seattle, Washington, in 1935.

3. The early B-17s required crews of six to nine men. The later F and G series had more machine guns and required a crew of ten.

In the summer of 1943 there weren't any facilities for the troops in Moses Lake. The whole air base was nothing but a headquarters building, a PX,[1] and a lot of tents. I didn't care. The base was only about forty miles south of Coulee City, so I thought I'd get to go home a lot as long as I was stationed there.

During the war, Moses Lake was one of the places where the Army was assembling flight crews for the B-17 bombers,[2] and there were guys coming in from all different parts of the country. I had to take a lot of teasing when they found out where I was from. Mostly, it was about the scenery around eastern Washington. "Hey, Dale," they'd say, "I thought this was supposed to be the 'Evergreen State.' So, where's all the trees?"

It took ten guys to make a B-17 crew. There were the pilot and copilot, a bombardier, a navigator, and six gunners.[3] I was one of the gunners. Our pilot's name was Mangis; the copilot was a fellow by the name of Lembcke. They were both pretty nice guys, I thought, but I never really got to know either of them very well.

Celusnak was our bombardier; his job was to operate the bombsight. He sat on a chair just inside the nose of the plane with the bombsight on a kind of a pedestal in front of him. This Norden bombsight we had was a real secret thing.⁴ We were all told it would be a disaster for the Allies if the Germans ever got hold of one. I never knew too much about it, except that it was some kind of a machine that told us exactly where we had to fly when we got to our target area and when to drop the bombs. I know the bombardier had to hand-carry it onto the plane right before each mission, and afterward he had to take it back to a secured warehouse.

Our navigator's name was Faragasso. He was up beside the bombardier, inside the nose of the plane, in front of the cockpit. He could operate the cheek guns if he had to. Those were the two machine guns that stuck out, one on each side of the plane's nose. In a combat situation, the navigator was like a seventh gunner, but the Army didn't classify him that way because his main job was navigating, and also, I suppose, because he was a commissioned officer.

The navigator, bombardier, pilot, and copilot—they were all commissioned officers. The rest of us—the gunners—we were noncommissioned officers. Commissioned officers were more highly educated than noncoms, as a rule. They weren't necessarily college graduates, but they scored higher on the Army's IQ tests. If you scored high enough, you could ask to go to OCS. That was Officer

Cockpit of a restored B-17

The Norden bombsight had a computing device that the bombardier programmed before each mission to automatically release bombs over a predetermined target. It was considered one of America's most valuable and secret weapons and could, in theory, "drop a bomb into a pickle barrel from four miles up." There was, in truth, nothing secret about the Norden by the time the United States entered the war, however, as a German-born American who had once worked for the Norden's inventor had given blueprints for the device to the Luftwaffe.

Dale Aldrich's B-17 crew consisted of ten men. Standing, left to right: Lt. M. W. Mangis, Oregon, pilot; Lt. D. F. Lembcke, New York, copilot; Lt. F. Faragasso, New York, navigator (replaced later by Lt. Jack Bennett, not pictured); Lt. L. J. Celusnak, Minnesota, bombardier. Kneeling, left to right: S/Sgt. W. R. Tracy, New York, engineer/dorsal turret or "Martin" gunner; S/Sgt. R. C. Dabney, Ohio, radio operator/gunner; Sgt. W. H. McMaster, Mississippi, armorer/waist gunner; Sgt. J. B. Short, Michigan, assistant radio operator/waist gunner; Sgt. D. W. Aldrich, Washington, assistant engineer/ball turret or "belly" gunner; Sgt. A. Svoboda, Illinois, assistant armorer/tail gunner.

Candidate School. I took the IQ tests when I was drafted—I think everybody did—but I never followed up on it to see if I might have qualified for OCS. It just never entered my mind.

I don't know if there was any written rule—it was just common knowledge that officers and noncoms weren't supposed to mix. They could go to different clubs, they lived in separate barracks, and they ate at separate messes. The whole crew worked together, sure, but the sergeant gunners rarely socialized with the pilot or any of the higher-ranking officers.

We gunners were the reason the plane was called a Flying Fortress. We had guns all over the plane—eleven altogether—all .50-caliber machine guns. Our job was to shoot at the enemy's fighter planes, to make it harder for them to get close enough to shoot us down. Each of us had a certain noncombat specialty, too, and that sort of dictated which of the six gunner positions you got assigned to.

At the very top of the plane, just above and behind the cockpit, there were two guns mounted on a turret. We called that the Martin.[5] The plane's engineer was usually the Martin gunner. In our crew that was Bill Tracy. Dick Dabney was our radio-operator gunner. He had his own little room inside the plane, with a door he could close if he needed to, to cut down on the noise. There was a desk in there with lots of radios all around it, and then Dabney had the one ring-mounted machine gun that stuck out from the top of the plane, between the bomb bay—that's where we stowed our bombs—and the "waist" section.

 The Martin was also known as the dorsal, or upper, turret.

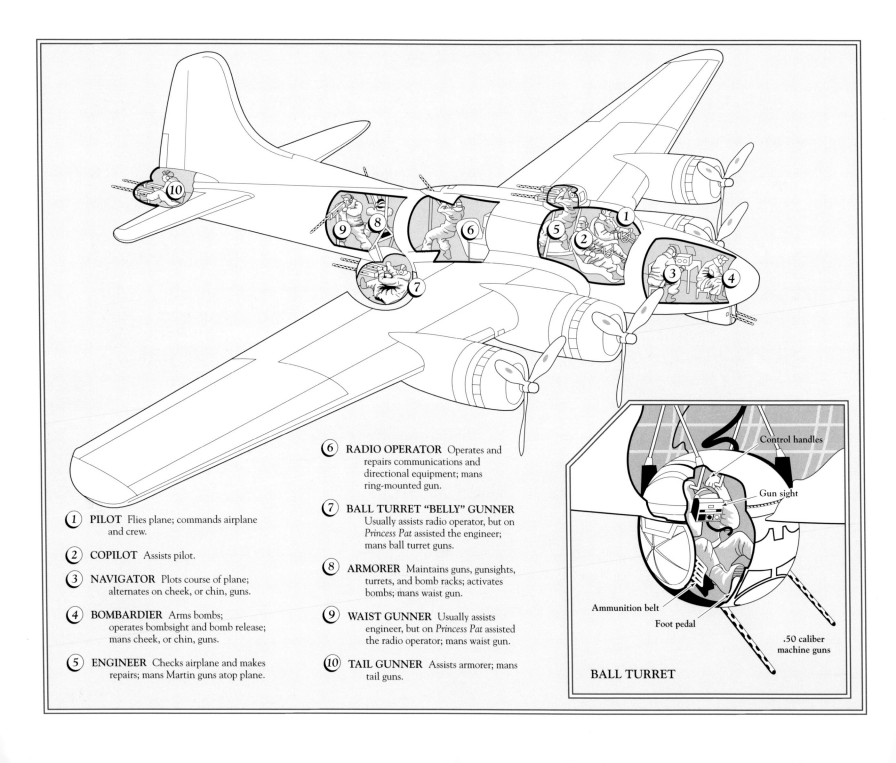

1 **PILOT** Flies plane; commands airplane and crew.

2 **COPILOT** Assists pilot.

3 **NAVIGATOR** Plots course of plane; alternates on cheek, or chin, guns.

4 **BOMBARDIER** Arms bombs; operates bombsight and bomb release; mans cheek, or chin, guns.

5 **ENGINEER** Checks airplane and makes repairs; mans Martin guns atop plane.

6 **RADIO OPERATOR** Operates and repairs communications and directional equipment; mans ring-mounted gun.

7 **BALL TURRET "BELLY" GUNNER** Usually assists radio operator, but on *Princess Pat* assisted the engineer; mans ball turret guns.

8 **ARMORER** Maintains guns, gunsights, turrets, and bomb racks; activates bombs; mans waist gun.

9 **WAIST GUNNER** Usually assists engineer, but on *Princess Pat* assisted the radio operator; mans waist gun.

10 **TAIL GUNNER** Assists armorer; mans tail guns.

Control handles

Gun sight

Ammunition belt

Foot pedal

.50 caliber machine guns

BALL TURRET

Radio room of a restored B-17G, located between the bomb bay and the waist section of the aircraft.

The bomb bay of a restored B-17G, located behind the cockpit, where bombs were stored "until it was time to open up the floor and drop them."

The waist is the middle of the airplane. You had to have two waist gunners because there were two windows in the waist, one on each side of the plane, and each window had a gun sticking out of it, mounted on brackets. One of the waist gunners had to be the armorer—the one that activates the bombs. The armorer for our crew was Bill McMaster. After we were in the air, Bill had to walk through the radio room and then step across a catwalk to get into the bomb bay—that's where our bombs hung on racks until it was

In 1942 the Air Force's nine-week course in air-craft armament was taught at Lowry Field in Denver, Colorado.

 Al Capone, also known as "Scarface," was a Chicago gangster and racketeer of the 1920s.

 A ball-shaped chamber underneath a plane where a gunner known as the ball turret, or "belly," gunner sits.

time to open up the floor and drop them. Then he had to cut the safety wires on all the fuses. Handling those bombs was pretty dangerous work, so all the gunners who did that had to go to a special armorers' school. Bill said he went to the one in Denver.[6] The other waist gunner was our assistant radio operator. His name was Jack Short.

There were two more guns sticking out the back of the plane, in the tail section. Those were for the tail gunner—that was Tony Svoboda—and he was also the assistant armorer. Tony was Italian, from the south side of Chicago, tough as they come. He told me his dad was in prison for being one of Al Capone's[7] henchmen. I don't know if that was really true or not. If the father was anything like his son, I think it probably was.

I was what they called the belly gunner, down inside the ball turret.[8] The ball turret looked kind of like a bubble on the underside of the plane. The only way to get into the ball while the plane was in the air was to go through a hole in the floor, right about in the middle of the waist. You had to open up the trapdoor on the ball itself and kind of slide yourself down into it.

Being inside the ball turret felt almost like sitting in a recliner chair, except the arms were connected to two machine guns. Whenever I needed to fire my guns, all I had to do was press the buttons with my thumbs. I had to aim with my feet on these two pedals. It took some practice, but I finally got so I could turn the whole ball turret in a full circle and shoot both guns in any direction I wanted. Except straight up, of course.

It wasn't a hard-and-fast rule, but it was customary for the assistant radio operator to be the belly gunner. In our crew, that would have been Jack Short. The trouble was, Jack was not short. He was more than six feet tall, so he couldn't fit very well inside the ball turret. Since I'd been to Air College and graduated as a mechanic, that made me the plane's assistant engineer. It also meant I should have been a waist gunner, and that's how we started out—me in the waist and Jack in the belly. We even tried flying that way a couple of times, but Jack said it was just too cramped down there for him. He wanted to trade places with me.

The ball turret was a pretty small space, but I was a lot shorter than Jack. It fit me just right. So that's why I ended up being the belly gunner instead of Jack. Our pilot was the one who decided we could go ahead and trade positions, but everybody in the crew agreed it was the right thing to do.[9]

I really liked it better down there in the belly anyway. It was a lot warmer, for one thing. I didn't have to stand in front of a big open window like the waist gunners did, and later on, when we started going on bombing missions, I found out I could just curl up and go to sleep until we got over our target.

We wore these heated flight suits with coils running all through them. They looked kind of like baby-blue-colored long johns, and they worked just like an electric blanket. You plugged your cord into one of the rheostats inside the plane, whichever one was closest, and then set the temperature you liked. Flight suits weren't very comfortable, but you had to have them to keep warm

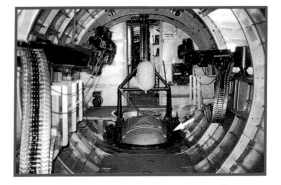

The ball turret as it appears from inside a Flying Fortress. Note the left and right waist guns, loaded for combat with .50 caliber machine gun cartridge belts.

 The ball turret gunner was almost always the smallest member of the crew.

Typically B-17s cruised at altitudes above 20,000 feet (6,100 meters) where temperatures ranged from -10° to -70°F (-23° to -57°C).

inside a plane with so many open windows.[10] During practices, if you went to sleep, somebody in the crew would turn up the rheostat on you and then everybody'd laugh when you woke up in a sweat. They couldn't reach me, though. I was all by myself, down in the belly.

As near as I could tell, once you got assigned to a crew the only purpose for being in Moses Lake was to let the pilots and copilots practice their takeoffs and landings. Nobody else had anything to do except get on and go along for the ride. For about three weeks in July, it seemed like that's all we did—taxi and take off, turn around in the air, and land again. Mangis and Lembcke had a tendency to use the brakes too much when they landed. That caused us a lot of tire blowouts the first few times; braking makes the tires real hot when they touch down on the runway.

All of the planes we flew in Moses Lake were B-17s, but I don't think any of the crews had any particular plane assigned to them. I know we didn't. And there was only one practice flight I remember for some reason. It was the Fourth of July, and we were flying over Sun Lakes [resort area in eastern Washington]. There wasn't any state park like there is now, but I could see a lot of cars and a whole bunch of people. It looked like everybody was having fun, all swimming and fishing. I remember wishing I was one of them.

My mom and dad drove over to visit me a few times while I was stationed in Moses Lake. Dad brought me my car. Ted Rice usually came with my parents. His family had a farm near Coulee City, and his father was one of my dad's best car customers. Ted's dad and mine were also pretty good friends, so when it came time for Ted to go to high school in Coulee City, Ted moved into our house in town and lived with us for four years because there weren't any school buses for the farm kids then. He was two years younger than me, but we were pretty close, almost like brothers.

I did get to go home quite a few times while I was in Moses Lake. It just depended on our practice schedule; sometimes we flew at night and sometimes during the day. If our crew got done by five or so in the afternoon, I'd get in my car and drive to Coulee City in time for dinner with my family and Ted. Then I'd go see my girlfriend. I never told her about Jackie.

Some time in August my crew got transferred to Walla Walla [Washington] for the last part of our training. That's where we started dropping bombs on a target from high altitudes. They weren't live bombs, just practice ones filled with some kind of white, powdery stuff. I'm not sure, but it might have been flour. I know our bombardier wasn't very good at it. He must have had trouble learning how to work the bombsight just right. Seemed like our bombs always landed too far away from the targets when we should have hit them dead-on.

Every now and then we'd take a trip to Sacramento, California, and different places in Oregon. That was for the navigator, to let him practice giving flight directions to the pilot and copilot. I remember one time I was sitting in the engineer's seat,[11] right behind the pilot in the cockpit. We'd just come out of some clouds, and I was looking out the window. All of a sudden there was a

 During takeoffs and landings, the gunner, who was designated as the plane's engineer, sat on a belt seat between the copilot and pilot to help monitor the gauges.

mountain, just under our right wing. The copilot must have seen it about the same time I did because he hollered at the pilot, and then Mangis pushed all four engine controls up as hard as he could. That pulled us just high enough to avoid crashing. We shouldn't have been that close to a mountain in the first place. Everybody knew it was the navigator's mistake; I guess we figured it was better to get it over with now rather than later, in combat.

We gunners got a little bit of practice in Walla Walla, too, but only at targets on the ground. The pilot would fly real low over some abandoned farm shed and let us shoot at that. I learned my left-foot pedal was for my gun sights. It felt like the clutch in my car. I also discovered my guns had a limit switch on them. Without that, I could have shot into the propellers. I even got to fly a B-17 once while we were in Walla Walla. I couldn't have landed it, but at least I knew how to fly the thing.

After we'd gone out on several training flights, the base commander ordered our whole crew to report to his office. He said he'd just received a report that all the morphine in our first-aid kit was missing, and he accused us of taking it. I knew we had a first-aid kit up by the cockpit, but I never knew what all was in it. I sure didn't know we had morphine. The pilot said he knew we had it, but he was totally dumbfounded as to why it was gone.

The CO kept us there in his office for quite a while, asking us every question he could think of. Probably he was just hoping he could scare one of us into confessing, but nobody did. Finally, he let us go. We never did find out who stole the morphine out of our first-aid kit. It could have been somebody in one of the ground crews, I guess. I was pretty sure it wasn't one of us. I hoped it wasn't.

One night in Walla Walla, all of us gunners went up to Bill McMaster's hotel room to meet his wife and kids. They'd come all the way from Mississippi to see him, so he was staying at the hotel with them as long as they were in town. I remember his wife was real upset, and rightfully so, as it turned out. She'd been reading the newspaper and saw an article about Regensburg [in central Germany].[12] Sixty bombers, all shot down in one day. I guess they ran into a lot of fighters and flak.[13] Bill's wife was all hysterical there in the hotel room, crying, saying she was afraid something like that might happen to us. It took a while for Bill and all of us to get her calmed down. It was a pretty bad scene, but I don't think it made us any more scared than we already were. We just figured we'd be lucky. Every soldier has to think that.

Finally, in September our crew was one of several that got picked to go by train to St. Louis. That was where bomber pilots had to go to take one final instrument test before they were allowed to fly in combat. Well, our pilot, Mangis, I guess he partied a little too much in St. Louis the night before the test and flunked it. I wasn't really mad at him for that. He felt real bad, and he told us all how sorry he was. And then I remember he said, "I guess this means we're all going to live a little longer." I didn't think too much about it at the time, but looking back on what he said then, I believe Mangis fully expected to die in combat.

If our pilot had passed his test, the Army probably would have shipped us directly from St. Louis to somewhere overseas right

 On August 17, 1943, B-17 bomber groups pushed deep into central Germany with the intention of destroying factories at Regensburg and Schweinfurt. The mission ended in a rout, with 60 out of 376 bombers being shot down. This was the first of many air-combat disasters known as the "autumn crisis" of 1943, when the entire U.S. policy of daylight bombing over Germany appeared to be a total failure.

 A contraction formed from the German word *Fliegerabwherkannon*, which means "antiaircraft fire from the ground."

Due to illness, transfers, and death in combat, it was rare for an entire bomber crew to serve a complete tour of duty together.

away. Since he didn't, we got orders to go back to Walla Walla for more training instead. We also got a new crew member. Another crew that was ready to go overseas needed a navigator. I don't know if theirs got sick or what happened to him, but they took ours. We got a new one, Jack Bennett, after we got back to Walla Walla.[14]

We had a little free time before we had to leave St. Louis, so we gunners decided to put on our leather flight jackets and go downtown. Flight jackets were made out of a real smooth leather, kind of a medium-brown color. There were wings on the shoulder patch, and you got a silver pin with wings on it that you wore over the left breast pocket. The pin was what told which member of the crew you were. The pilot had a special insignia between the wings on his pin; the bombardier had a bomb. The gunners' insignia was a bullet with wings on it.

They were really nice jackets, very comfortable to wear, and we liked them. Flight jackets were what distinguished us as fliers. Nobody else had them.

Well, just when we were about to go downtown, Celusnak, the bombardier, told us we couldn't wear our jackets because they weren't our "Class A" uniforms. Class A uniforms were our khakis, with a shirt and tie. I never did like Celusnak very much. He was always trying to give us noncoms orders. Usually we didn't listen to him. We figured the pilot was in charge of our crew, even though he and the bombardier were both the same rank, which was second lieutenants. Mangis said he didn't care if we wanted to wear our flight jackets, so we went ahead and wore them.

I'd been planning to see Jackie before I had to leave for Walla Walla. I did call her several times while I was there. We just couldn't seem to work it out. Whenever I was free, she couldn't get away from her job. I called her again just before I had to leave. Well, then she was babysitting for her two younger sisters. I said, "Bring them along." So she loaded them in her car and drove all the way out to the airport to see me. It was a pretty short visit, and we couldn't really talk with her sisters there.

Jackie was upset, but it didn't bother me much. I figured I'd see her again pretty soon. Mangis was going to have to retake the pilot's test, so I knew the whole crew would be in St. Louis at least once more before we left the States. I was wrong. Mangis did have to go back to St. Louis all right—and he passed his test—but the rest of the crew didn't get to go with him the second time.

We trained for three more weeks with our new navigator in Walla Walla. Finally, we got orders for the whole crew to travel by train to Camp Kilmer, New Jersey. We knew that meant we were about to go overseas, probably to Europe, probably to bomb the Germans. We'd practiced a lot. By that time we were anxious to get into the war.

The leather jackets issued to American flight crews during World War II were highly prized. Here a student models one from the Confederate Air Force Museum in Mesa, Arizona.

CROSSING THE ATLANTIC

We were only at Camp Kilmer for a couple of days in late October before we got orders to board the *Queen Elizabeth*. The *Queen Elizabeth* was a luxury ocean liner, like the cruise ships they have now. During the war the British government converted it to a transport ship, and that was how a lot of the troops got to England.

The Army said there were 15,000 of us on board. That was way more than the ship's usual capacity, so they just took out all the nice furniture and put three bunk beds in each stateroom for the soldiers, except for the infantry soldiers, mostly Puerto Ricans. They all slept outside, on the top deck of the ship.

I don't think the Puerto Ricans had to sleep outside because of racism. I think it was because you got your quarters assigned according to your order of boarding, and that was determined by your rank. The Puerto Ricans were infantry soldiers, so they must have been outranked by everybody else on the ship. Our com-

The luxury liner Queen Elizabeth carried troops overseas during World War II.

To prevent American troops and supplies from reaching England, the Germans patrolled the Atlantic in "wolf" packs of eight to twenty submarines.

The surface speed of a German U-boat (submarine) was 17 knots (on diesel power); submerged speed was 7 or 8 knots (on batteries). Converted liners like the *Queen Mary* and the *Queen Elizabeth*, had maximum speeds of 26 knots.

A British physicist first developed radar for practical use in 1935. By World War II the United States, Germany, and France had independently developed radar for navigation and location purposes.

mander told us they were a pretty tough bunch of guys, and it seemed like he admired them for that. But he also cautioned us not to go up to the top deck at all. "You go up there with those guys," he said, "and you might not come back."

Sometime during the trip to England, I heard what happened to my repair squadron—the guys I worked with when I was still an aircraft mechanic back in San Antonio. Apparently they got transferred overseas, too, but the ship they were on got torpedoed and sunk by a German sub.[1] I don't know if any of them got rescued or not. I probably would have been with them if I hadn't volunteered for gunnery school when I did.

The *Queen Elizabeth* was supposed to be safer than any of the other ships that were going across the Atlantic because it could travel so much faster than a submarine.[2] I'm not sure if the German subs had radar,[3] but even if they did, they couldn't have caught up with us. It still took us four or five days to get from New Jersey to England, though, because of all the zigzagging we had to do. Our ship could outrun a sub all right, but if we had kept to a straight course all the way across the ocean, the Germans would have been able to predict where to find us at any given point in time.

Every time we made one of those sudden zigzag turns, the tables in the mess hall would go sliding across the room. One poor guy got his leg broken when a table came by and crushed him up against a wall. You really had to hang on to something whenever there was a sharp turn like that.

I was about halfway seasick the whole trip, so I was pretty glad when I finally got off that boat in Liverpool [port city in northwest England]. That was the third of November.

From Liverpool they put us on a train and took us to a fairly good-size city called Newcastle upon Tyne. I don't remember much about the trip after that, except there was a lot of getting on and off trains. That went on for several days until we finally ended up in a town called Horham [seventy-five miles east of London].[4] It was just a real nice, quiet little country village, or, I should say, that's what it would have been if it weren't for this great big American air base on the outskirts of the town.

 Horham, pronounced HOR-um, was one of many English cities that hosted American air bases during World War II. Except for neutral Sweden, Switzerland, Spain, Portugal, and Ireland, Great Britain was the only European country never conquered or occupied by Germany.

HORHAM AIR BASE

Bomber groups were composed of four squadrons consisting of eight to fourteen planes per squadron. The U.S. Eighth Air Force had twenty-nine different bomber groups flying B-17s from British air bases. The 95th Bomber Group was formed in September 1942 at Geiger Field, Spokane, Washington.

By mid-1943, the chance of completing a tour of twenty-five missions was little better than one in three.

We arrived at Horham Air Base on November the ninth. That was the home of the 95th Bomber Group.[1] We were assigned to the 335th Squadron; I'd guess we were one of at least a hundred B-17 crews at that base. When they took us to our barracks, some of the guys who'd been there a while told us we were replacing a crew that had all been killed in an explosion on the runway the week before. Runway accidents as bad as that were pretty rare, so that didn't bother us too much. We did talk about it once in a while, which maybe helped us get over being nervous, but we all knew every time you took off there was a chance you wouldn't make it.

We also knew if you flew twenty-five bombing missions and survived, you could go home.[2] I talked to a few guys from other crews who were close to that many; I never met anybody who actually made it. I heard there was one crew that got their twenty-five, but then they crashed into a mountain right there in England when they were on their way home. We thought we would make twenty-five. The chances were not good, but we had to believe it was possible.

There was never too much socializing with other crews in the barracks. There was a lot of turnover, for one thing, as crews were being shot down and replaced all the time. Also, we weren't supposed to talk with anyone outside our own crew about our mission targets or anything related to our missions for security reasons. It was pretty well understood you had to keep your missions secret because the Germans had spies everywhere. I heard one time a guy from one of the crews at Horham got drunk and talked about a mission. That caused the Germans to be ready for them with more fighters than they would've ordinarily had in the target area.

Every crew had its own plane assigned to them, and all the planes had names. Ours was the *Princess Pat*. It was named after my sister, Patsy Joy Aldrich; our pilot's wife was also named Pat. Some crews named their planes after the women who worked in the factories that built them.[3] The women would write their names, addresses, and phone numbers on a little slip of paper and stick it in a certain place in the plane's control column for the pilots to find. All the pilots knew right where to look for those girls' phone numbers in the cockpit. I don't know if Mangis found one in the *Princess Pat*. He never said.

This was the first time we'd ever had any particular plane assigned to us. The *Princess Pat* was a brand-new B-17, and I remember it was a "G."[4] It looked to be about the same size as the

Sgt. Dale Aldrich at Horham Air Base, England, November 1943, wearing full mission gear, including leather helmet and sheepskin jacket.

 During the war millions of American women joined the workforce for the first time, taking jobs in factories and offices previously held by their fathers, sons, brothers, and husbands who were in the service. Some worked in aircraft plants.

 A letter identified each new series of B-17s. The B-17G was the last and most numerous of the Flying Fortresses used during the war. To keep up with demand, Boeing subcontracted the production of approximately half of the Fs and Gs to its two major competitors, Lockheed and Douglas. By April 1944, the three companies reached a peak output of sixteen planes per day.

The B-17G had thirteen machine guns, but the extra guns were operated by the bombardier and did not require an additional gunner.

 Bombing missions from England to targets in western Europe and back took four to six hours; for missions into central Germany, eight to ten.

planes we trained on in Moses Lake and Walla Walla; the wingspan must have been at least a hundred feet. I know the ball turret was the same. The plane had a little different paint job, though—kind of an olive drab for camouflage instead of the plain metal we were used to seeing on the trainers. Other than that, the only difference I could see was that they added a chin turret with two more machine guns right below the nose.[5] I guess the bombardier could have used the chin turret guns if he had to, but during a mission he was really too busy operating the bombsight to help defend the plane.

Horham is located inland, in the southern part of England. Bombing missions from there usually went over the English Channel and on to whatever the target happened to be that day. Some bombing missions were considered milk runs, more or less. A milk run meant it was a shorter one, say, to France, or Belgium, or Holland. If you were on a milk run, it meant you were in the air less time, which reduced the amount of time you were at risk of being shot down.[6]

We weren't told we were about to go on our first mission until after dinner the night before. It was the pilot's job to tell us. I don't remember being especially nervous that night. I think we were all scared, all the time, but you always think you're not the one. There were some guys who just gave up to the fear. They just said they couldn't do it, and then the Army would let them go. They got assigned to office work or supply-depot duty instead.

I remember praying that if I was going to die the next day, that it be quick. I never made a will, because I didn't have anything to will. Just my car. I had a '34 Ford two-door. After I left home my dad put it up on blocks beside our house. He told me while I was gone Mike [a friend] came over and asked if he could buy it. I had only paid two hundred dollars for that car, but there weren't any new cars to buy during the war so Mike offered my dad four hundred dollars for it.[7] He even said he'd give it back to me for nothing when I came home. Dad still told him no. He said it was because he didn't trust Mike, and that he just wanted to be damn sure that car was there for me when I got back. I guess he got a lot of other offers, too, but he refused them all. Dad never told me he was afraid I might not come home, but that car really was the only thing I had to leave him. Maybe that was why he told everybody it wasn't for sale.

I don't remember the exact date of that first mission, but I'm sure it was in November. The pilot came into the barracks real early in the morning and woke us up. It must have been about 3:00 A.M. I know none of us had slept much because we'd all gone over to the Red Cross for beer the night before, and then we'd sat up late and talked about girls.

We always got a special breakfast on the morning of a bombing mission. They gave us ham or bacon and real eggs instead of the usual powdered ones. That was really good. There was usually some bread to go with it, and orange marmalade and peanut butter.

After breakfast, we'd go to another building for the mission briefing. You might see anywhere from fifty to one hundred gunners in the room, depending on how many squadrons were going. There was a map on the wall with a sheet draped over it for secu-

 From February 1942 until the end of the war, all car manufacture ceased as manufacturers retooled to produce parts and vehicles for the military.

On a typical daylight bombing mission over Germany, the B-17s flew in formation, often meeting fierce resistance from German artillery on the ground and fighter planes in the sky

rity. Pretty soon an officer would come in and pull the sheet off. Everybody'd look real hard then, to see where the string was. The purpose of the string was to show where we were supposed to fly that day, the most direct route from Horham to the target. Then another briefing officer would come in and tell us how much flak we could expect and how many fighters they thought the Germans were going to send up.

Our pilot went to a different briefing, the one for higher-ranking officers, so it was his job to tell us if there was anything else we needed to know. Mangis generally did give us a few more details. He'd talk to the whole crew over the intercom, after we were in the air.

I don't remember the exact destinations of the first or second mission—just that we were bombing somewhere over Europe—but the third one was to Emden [Germany]. Mangis said Emden was a seaport where the Germans had some sub pens.[8] He also told us if we could put a few of those subs out of business, it would really help the Allies.

I never saw the bombs being loaded on the plane. The ground crew took care of that sometime during the night. I know the bombs were already in the bomb bay by the time we got to the runway. The number of bombs varied according to the mission; I think we usually had about ten.[9] However many there were, right after we took off the bombardier had to go around and take the safety pins out of all the fuses.

The first part of every mission was to get into our formation[10] over England. That always took a while, maybe an hour or more,

 A reinforced concrete structure used by the Germans to shelter submarines while they were in port for refueling, rearming, or repairs.

 Loaded with 2 to 3 tons (1.8 to 2.7 metric tons) of bombs and 8 tons (7.3 metric tons) of fuel, the typical mission weight for a B-17G was about 10 tons (9.1 metric tons). The bomb load was less for long flights and more for short ones, as the distance to the target determined how much weight had to be allocated for the fuel.

 Beginning in March 1943, American bombers flew in a "combat box" formation. This consisted of three groups of twenty-one planes each, staggered so that no plane was directly above or below another. Later, when long-range fighters began providing escort protection, this formation was no longer necessary.

depending on how many planes there were; I think there must have been at least a hundred every time. I usually just took a nap. The other guys couldn't figure out how I could go to sleep. They were all excited, I guess, and so was I, but they were cold, too, and I wasn't. I was all nice and warm down there in the belly, and there was nothing else for me to do until the whole formation was crossing the English Channel. That was when I'd hear the pilot come on over the earphones in my helmet. He'd say, "Check your guns," and that was what woke me up.

Pretty soon after we were across the Channel, Mangis would come on again and say, "They're blinking their lights at us!" That meant the German fighter planes were firing their guns. By that time I could see them, too. When they shot at us, it looked just like the headlights on a car flashing on and off, and it seemed like they were all around us.[11] I shot back, and I just kept shooting until I didn't see them anymore.

I don't know if any American or British fighter planes went with us on any of the first three bombing missions. They could have been there, far ahead or high above us. In the heat of battle you might not see them at all, or at least I never did.

I heard there were times when gunners accidentally shot down American fighter planes. I couldn't understand how that might happen until I saw what air combat was really like. It's pretty confusing up there, and it's hard to tell one fighter plane from another when they're swarming all around you. They'd come in and go by us so fast, sometimes all you could see was a blur. That's why I never shot at anything that wasn't shooting at me first.[12]

 In 1943, the Luftwaffe usually attacked B-17 formations with groups of twenty to thirty fighter planes.

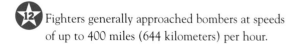 Fighters generally approached bombers at speeds of up to 400 miles (644 kilometers) per hour.

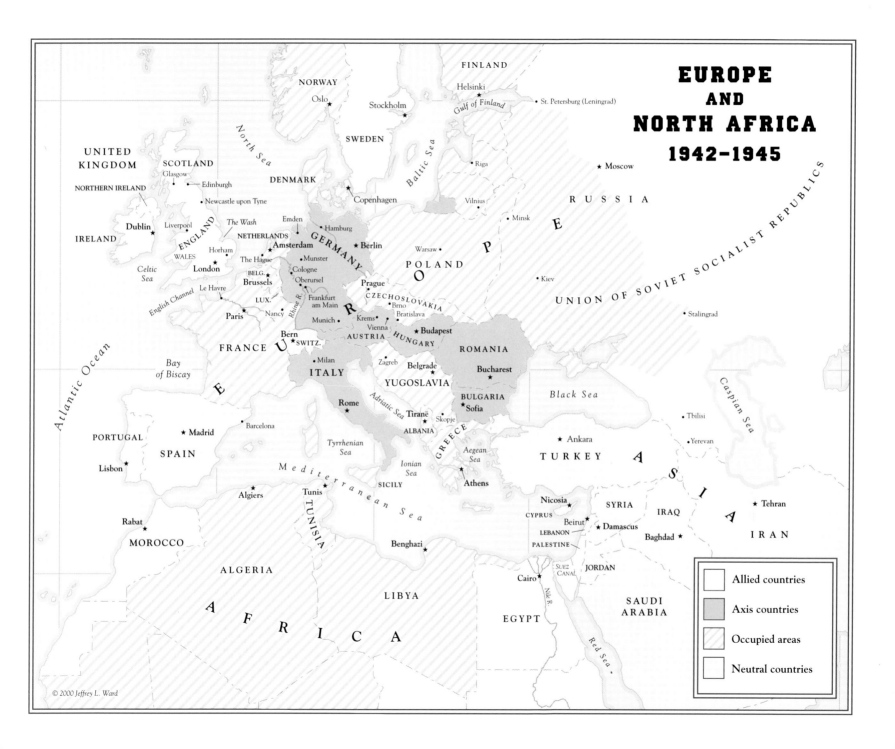

EUROPE
AND
NORTH AFRICA
1942–1945

FINLAND

NORWAY
Oslo ★

Helsinki
Stockholm

• St. Petersburg (Leningrad)

Gulf of Finland

SWEDEN

North Sea

Baltic Sea

• Riga

★ Moscow

UNITED
KINGDOM

SCOTLAND
Glasgow •
• Edinburgh

DENMARK

RUSSIA

• Vilnius

• Minsk

NORTHERN IRELAND
• Newcastle upon Tyne

Copenhagen

★ Berlin

• Hamburg

Emden •

IRELAND
Dublin ★

Liverpool •

The Wash

Warsaw •

POLAND

UNION OF SOVIET SOCIALIST REPUBLICS

ENGLAND

NETHERLANDS
Amsterdam ★

Munster •

GERMANY

• Kiev

WALES
Horham •

The Hague •

Celtic
Sea

London ★

BELG. •
Brussels ★

Cologne •
Oberursel •

Prague ★

CZECHOSLOVAKIA

• Stalingrad

Le Havre •

English Channel

LUX. •

Frankfurt
am Main

Rhine R.

Brno •
• Bratislava

Paris ★

Nancy •

Munich •

Krems •

Bern ★
★ SWITZ.

AUSTRIA

Vienna •

★ Budapest

HUNGARY

ROMANIA

FRANCE

U
R
O
P
E

Bay
of Biscay

Atlantic Ocean

• Milan

ITALY

Zagreb •

Belgrade ★

YUGOSLAVIA

★ Bucharest

BULGARIA
★ Sofia

Black Sea

Caspian Sea

Tyrrhenian
Sea

Rome ★

Adriatic Sea

Tiranë ★

Skopje •

ALBANIA

GREECE

Aegean
Sea

• Tbilisi

★ Ankara

• Yerevan

TURKEY

A
S
I
A

PORTUGAL

SPAIN

• Madrid ★

• Barcelona

Ionian
Sea

SICILY

Athens ★

Mediterranean Sea

Nicosia •

SYRIA

Lisbon ★

Algiers •

Tunis •

TUNISIA

CYPRUS
Beirut ★

IRAQ

★ Tehran

Damascus ★

Rabat •

Benghazi •

LEBANON

Baghdad •

PALESTINE

IRAN

MOROCCO

ALGERIA

A   F   R   I   C   A

LIBYA

Cairo •

Nile R.

SUEZ
CANAL

JORDAN

EGYPT

SAUDI
ARABIA

Red Sea

	Allied countries
	Axis countries
	Occupied areas
	Neutral countries

© 2000 Jeffrey L. Ward

I don't know how many German fighter planes I shot down. I don't even know if I actually hit any of them. I saw a few go down, but there were a lot of other bombers all flying in the same formation, and we were all shooting at the same fighter planes. There was no way to tell which gunner was responsible for which kill, so I'm not sure if anybody in my crew could have claimed he shot down a certain number of Germans on any mission. Some bomber crews tried to keep a running count of their kills, but individual crew members didn't, so far as I know. The only thing we kept track of was the number of missions we flew. After we got back, the ground crews painted little bombs on the nose of the plane, one for each mission.[13]

 A practice borrowed from the British.

B-17 crews painted a little symbol (usually a bomb) on the nose of their aircraft after each bombing raid.

It seemed like we'd been in the air forever, but it was usually about noon when we got back from a bombing raid. The Red Cross gave us coffee and doughnuts; the officers had to go somewhere for debriefing. I was never debriefed, but the pilot told us it was just to find out what happened during the mission and to report if they saw anything unusual. I was always too tensed up to go back to the barracks and sleep, so sometimes I'd go to one of the pubs for a sandwich and a beer. Other times I'd just walk around the base or ride a bike—whatever I could do to relax.

Bombing missions were usually a week apart. The crew had to rest. It was physically and emotionally hard to perform at peak efficiency during a mission. Also, the plane had to be checked for maintenance and repairs after every mission. Sometimes, if the weather was too bad, missions got called off.

We were always scared we were going to be the first crew to try daylight bombing[14] over Berlin. That was the most dangerous mission we could think of. You could see the target better in the daylight, but that meant the German fighter planes could see us better, too. Sure enough, our crew was actually scheduled to be among the first to bomb Berlin in daylight. We just didn't know it until after the mission was canceled. We were told it got called off due to a breach of security, but I don't really know for sure.[15]

Between missions, we could go to The Wash. The Wash was not an air base; it was the name of a bay and also a tourist resort over on the east coast of England, on the North Sea. The Army just took it over for the troops during the war, and you could ask to be sent there for further training. Everybody knew it was really just

 The British did all their bombing at night, and so did the Americans, at first. Later, the Americans shifted to daylight bombings. Although these missions were dangerous, the Americans believed they allowed greater accuracy and thus were worth the risks.

 The first major daylight bombing raid on Berlin was delayed until March 1944 because U.S. fighters lacked the capacity to carry enough fuel to accompany the bombers all the way to Germany and back. The losses at Schweinfurt and Regensburg proved to the Americans that their bombers could not penetrate into central Germany without fighter plane escorts, so the Americans limited their daylight bombing to targets in occupied countries (France, Belgium, Holland) or western Germany. Meanwhile, American factories worked overtime to build large numbers of fighters with enough range to escort the bombers deep into Germany.

a place you could go for R and R. I went once for two or three days in early December. The weather was way too cold at that time of year, so I didn't go down to the beach. There weren't any girls, the living quarters were ordinary barracks, and the food was just regular mess. I did attend a couple of classes on enemy aircraft recognition, but mainly I just went to The Wash to get a change of scenery.

I only went into town a couple of times. Every time I went, there'd be an air raid. When we heard the sirens, we found out we had just enough time to leave one pub and duck into the air-raid shelter of the next one down the street. I didn't get to town much during the day at all, but I hoped to go to London over Christmas and do a little sightseeing with Ralph Jorgensen.

Ralph was a friend of mine from Coulee City. We'd been writing letters back and forth for quite a while, so I knew he was a mechanic at some air base in England. Neither of us ever knew exactly where the other one was, though, so we just sent letters to our hometown addresses and let the Army forward them to wherever we happened to be stationed at the time.

Ralph and I had big plans. We were going to meet at Piccadilly Circus in the middle of downtown London on Christmas Eve. Ralph told me he was there, all right, and he said he waited and waited for me until he finally decided I wasn't coming. He said he knew I wouldn't have stood him up on purpose, so that's when he figured something must have happened to me.

COINCIDING DATES
DURING ALDRICH'S HORHAM DUTY, EARLY NOVEMBER TO LATE DECEMBER 1943, THE ALLIES STEPPED UP THEIR BOMBING MISSIONS AND PLANNED TO INVADE EUROPE THROUGH FRANCE. (SEE TIMELINE.)

THE MÜNSTER MISSION

There wasn't too much discussion that morning. The pilot just said, "We're going to Münster [port city in western Germany and a key railroad center]." We'd all seen the string on the map. Everybody knew this was going to be anything but a milk run.

Münster was deeper into enemy territory than we'd ever flown before, inside Germany itself. The main trouble was, we were going to have to fly over Holland to get there. We'd be in the air over land for a long time. That meant longer exposure to flak and enemy fighter planes, a greater chance of getting shot down. It was almost as dangerous as going to Berlin, because the distance we would be over enemy territory was nearly the same. Münster just wasn't quite as heavily defended as Berlin.

It was December 22, 1943, our fourth bombing mission. I remember when we were still in the barracks that morning, putting on our gear and getting ready to ride out to the runway, one of the guys said, "I don't think I want to go on this one. It's my birthday, you know." He was just kidding around, but it really was his twenty-first birthday. That was Jack Short.

Right before we took off, I handed my sidearm to the ground-crew chief. That was always the last thing I did before a bombing mission. It was a Colt .45. I usually wore it in a shoulder holster, but nobody except the bombardier was supposed to take a sidearm on the plane. I guess that was so he could protect the bombsight. Even if we crashed, if he survived, I think he might have had instructions to either destroy it or defend it with his life.

I'm not sure why the rest of us couldn't wear our sidearms when we were on a mission. All they ever told us was, "You can't hold off a whole German army with one gun." I heard there'd been some incidents, times when guys went crazy and shot themselves or somebody else in the crew. I never talked to anybody who'd actually been there when anything like that happened, so maybe it was just rumors. Anyway, that was the rule, so I always gave my gun to the ground chief. My wallet, too. I told him if anything happened to me he could go through it and keep the cash or anything else he wanted, as long as he mailed the rest of it back to my parents. He promised he would.

It took a while for us to get into our slot in the formation. I'm not sure how many Fortresses were going altogether; it looked like at least a hundred or more. So far as I knew we were all on the same mission. I don't know if that was unusual or not, because I never really got to talk to anybody outside my own crew.[1]

 By late 1943 bomber formations consisted of hundreds of planes. Within a formation, the target was usually the same, regardless of number.

Our altitude was about 25,000 feet. I know the Germans had radar for spotting air traffic, but they probably didn't need it to see which way we were headed. All they had to do was look up and see our contrails.[2]

I remember seeing antiaircraft flak. If you're on the ground, the flak looks white. If you're looking down on it from inside a plane, it's black. It was like flying through a black curtain. I didn't have any open windows down in the ball turret, so I couldn't hear the shells exploding. There had to have been a lot of them to create all the flak I saw that day.

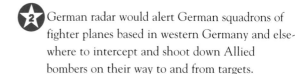 German radar would alert German squadrons of fighter planes based in western Germany and elsewhere to intercept and shoot down Allied bombers on their way to and from targets.

I couldn't see how the Germans could have missed hitting us. Either they were really poor shots, or else the shells were exploding on their own before they could reach our altitude. It was possible for the enemy to adjust the altitude of their antiaircraft shell explosions, but we believed their upper limit was 28,000 feet. That was why we always tried to stay above that.

It must have been about noon when we started to notice we were having trouble keeping up with our formation. The superchargers on two of our four engines weren't working right, and we were losing altitude. I knew our plane didn't get the usual maintenance and repair that week because another crew had needed it for a mission just a couple of days before. I don't know for sure, but that might have been the reason our engines were giving us so much trouble that day.

The plane just kept losing altitude until we finally had to drop out of the formation altogether, somewhere over northern Germany. I don't know what happened to the rest of our formation. I never found out how many of them made it to Münster or if the mission was successful.[3] Right then all I knew was we were going to have to turn around and try to get our plane and ourselves back to England in one piece.

We found we could fly just fine at around five thousand feet. But we needed to drop our bombs to make the flying easier and put less strain on the engines.

I'm not sure if we were still over Germany at that point, but there was no flak coming at us from the ground. I didn't see any towns below us, not even farmhouses. There was nothing but farm-

 Despite sometimes staggering losses of planes and crews, the Fortress formations were never turned back by enemy action.

land, so we ended up dropping all our bombs on some poor farmer's field. Turnips, probably, or rutabagas. I saw the bomb-bay doors open up, and I watched the bombs falling. I saw the smoke from the explosions when they hit the ground.

I felt real bad about that, dropping those bombs over a civilian area instead of our target. There was nothing else we could have done. We had to lighten our load to give ourselves the best chance of getting back to England. Besides, we never could have landed back at Horham or anywhere else with a full load of bombs. They probably would have exploded on the runway.

I was still looking down at the ground, watching our bombs exploding, when I saw some fighter planes go by. They were ours. I'm pretty sure I saw a couple of P-47s.[4] The others were definitely P-38s. You could always tell a P-38, even from a distance, just by looking at its tail.[5] Others, you had to wait until they were close enough to see their markings. Ours had stars; the Germans' had black crosses on the wings and swastikas on the tails. If you really wanted to be sure, you could wait until they started firing at you.

These were definitely ours. They flew right underneath me, so I could see their markings.[6] They had probably been up ahead, escorting our formation, but I don't think they could have gone all the way to Münster. I know they were starting to increase the fighter planes' range a little more by that time; some of them had drop tanks[7] with extra fuel under their wings. That let them fly a little farther, but the pilots had to drop them whenever they got into combat, so they still didn't have enough fuel to stay with us all the way into Germany and back. I never saw, never even heard

P-47

P-38

[4] The single-engine Republic P-47 Thunderbolt and the twin-engine Lockheed P-38 Lightning were, until early 1944, the best and most often used protective escort for America's heavy bombers.

[5] The twin tail and engine of the P-38 was an easily distinguished feature, known to the Germans as *der Gabelschwanzteufel*, which means "forked-tail devil."

[6] To avoid misidentification, American and British fighter pilots approached any B-17 slowly and cautiously, often tilting their wings to show their shapes and markings to the gunners.

[7] Drop tanks increased flight range by 50 percent or so, but also slowed the fighters and increased their risk of being incinerated if hit.

The P-51 Mustangs were the first American fighter planes with enough range to escort a bomber formation all the way to and from targets inside Germany. But the first mission using P-51s as bomber escorts did not occur until February 1944, nearly two months after Aldrich's mission to Münster.

P-51

 While such stories were just hearsay, the Germans sometimes used captured B-17s to follow formations and direct their fighters to the location of any stragglers.

All American and British planes and ships during World War II carried an IFF (Identification, Friend or Foe) device—a coded radar beacon.

about the P-51s.[8] Those must have come into the war later, after my time.

I heard one of the fighter pilots talking to Mangis over the radio. He knew we were in trouble, but the fighters were running out of fuel and had to get back to England right away. They couldn't stay with us any longer. I heard somebody say, "Good luck," and I remember looking down at them through my gun sights as they went by. I almost felt like shooting at them myself because they were going the wrong way. That was when I realized we were going to have to fend for ourselves.

Not long after the fighters left us, another B-17 like ours came along, and I heard Mangis say, "We'll fly with him." Then it disappeared into the clouds. It might have been one of ours, or it might have been one of ours that had been captured by the Germans. We'd heard stories of captured B-17s joining a formation and then just starting to shoot.[9]

You could usually identify any B-17 by the letter on its tail. That told which bomber group the plane belonged to. Ours had a "B." I also heard there was some kind of device in the radio that could identify whether another B-17 was friend or foe, but I wasn't sure if that was true.[10] I still don't know about that lone B-17 we flew beside for a little while that day. Its pilot didn't talk to us, and it never came close enough for me to see its tail letter.

I heard our navigator giving Mangis flight directions to Sweden. Sweden was a neutral country during the war; we could have gone there to land. From where we were at the time, it was probably a little farther than to England, but we had our "Tokyo tanks"—one on each wing for extra fuel. We called them Tokyo tanks because a B-17 was supposed to be able to fly all the way to Japan on them. That was probably just an exaggeration, but you could fly pretty far.[11] Tokyo tanks weren't usually filled unless you were going to need them for extra distance; it just depended on how far away the bombing target was. I know when we left for Münster that morning, our Tokyo tanks were full.

If we'd gone to Sweden, we would have been interned. We all had our suspicions that a lot of guys did that on purpose, just high-tailed it to Sweden whenever they got the chance so they could just sit and wait out the war. Mangis said, "No, we can make it back to England from here," and I thought he was right. We really could have made it.[12]

We almost did.

 The Tokyo tanks, available for the B-17Fs and Gs, could add as much as a thousand miles to a bomber's normal mission range.

 Of the approximately 11,500 B-17 crews that served in Europe and Africa during World War II, only 140 made emergency landings in neutral Sweden or Switzerland and were interned.

COINCIDING DATES

AT THE TIME OF ALDRICH'S MÜNSTER MISSION, DECEMBER 22, 1943, THE GERMAN SIEGE OF LENINGRAD WAS UNDERWAY AND MANY RUSSIANS WERE DYING OF STARVATION. MEANWHILE ALLIED PROGRESS IN ITALY WAS AT A STANDSTILL AND AMERICANS WERE MEETING STIFF RESISTANCE AT GUADALCANAL IN THE PACIFIC. (SEE TIMELINE.)

SHOT DOWN

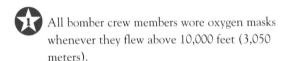

1 All bomber crew members wore oxygen masks whenever they flew above 10,000 feet (3,050 meters).

2 A B-17G's top speed was 287 miles (462 kilometers) per hour at 25,000 feet (7,625 meters).

Ju-88

3 Originally designed and used as a dive bomber, the Ju-88 was also deployed as a fighter plane.

Our engines were fine as long as we stayed around five thousand feet. Flying that low, I didn't need my oxygen mask[1] anymore, so I took it off. Our speed was pretty good, too—about two hundred miles an hour.[2] We flew like that for quite a while—at least a half an hour, I think—after we dropped out of our formation. I was starting to think maybe we were going to get lucky and make it all the way back to England, until the Germans finally picked us up.

They could have found us on radar, I suppose, but most likely some of their planes were just returning to their bases. Or maybe they were out looking for stragglers in that area when they saw us. I don't know how many fighters there were—too many to count. It might have been a whole squadron. All I know is they were coming in fast from all directions, and all of them were shooting at us.

I recognized some of them were Ju-88s—we called them Junkers.[3] I saw some Messerschmitts, too, and I'm pretty sure they were 109s.[4] I started shooting back at them, but I couldn't see how many we shot down. I was having trouble seeing anything because my glasses were all fogged up.

The Germans made at least two or three passes at us. One of them must have made a direct hit on our number four, which was our right engine. Only a direct hit could have caused a fire like that. The engineer—that was Bill Tracy—he said he thought it must have been a rocket to do that much damage.[5]

A few seconds after that, Mangis came on over the earphones and said, "Prepare to bail out!" I could see our right wing was on fire. That was where our fuel was, in the wing tanks, so I knew I had to get out of that plane in a hurry. I grabbed for my chest parachute and snapped it onto the front of my harness. I kept my parachute harness on all the time whenever I flew, but the parachute itself was too bulky to wear down in the belly-gunner's position. I could have taken my "Mae West"—that was this inflatable life jacket we all had—and the rubber dinghy, too. I kept both of those folded up and stuffed on a shelf above my head, right next to my parachute, but I didn't think I needed them because we weren't over water.

I had to turn my guns straight down at the ground to get out of the ball turret. That was the only way I could open the trapdoor above my head and pull myself up into the waist section while the plane was still in the air. The first thing I noticed was the door to the radio compartment. It was still closed. I don't know what made me open the door, but I did. That's when I saw Dabney was still in there, still shooting at the fighter planes. In all the commotion, I

Me-109

 The Me-109 was a single-seat fighter plane that first appeared in 1942. Its top speed was 425 miles (684 kilometers) per hour.

 Both the Ju-88 and the Me-109 were known to carry rockets.

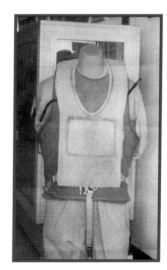

This World War II life jacket was known as a "Mae West" because, when inflated, it was said to resemble the figure of the famous 1930s and 40s blonde film star of that name.

guess he didn't hear the pilot's order. I yelled at him, "Come on, Dabney! Bail out!" and then I saw him stop shooting and head toward the bomb bay. That was where his emergency door was, but I didn't actually see him bail out.

Then I turned around and walked past the waist gunners. They should have been gone by that time, but I could tell by the way they were cupping their hands over their ear mikes that they were having trouble hearing. I was pretty certain they had not heard the bail-out command, so I waved at them to get their attention. They both looked at me, and I'm sure they must have seen me. I hollered at them, too: "Come on!" as loud as I could. I don't know if either one heard me.

Then I heard this big explosion, and I saw both of those guys get shot in the head. I think it must have been a 20-mm cannon,[6] because it tore part of their heads off, right above their eyebrows. I was standing right next to them, in the same line of fire, but they were tall guys—both over six feet. If I'd have been as tall as they were, I'm sure I'd have got it, too. Being only five-feet six is all that kept me out of the way of that cannon shell. As it was, I just got powder burns on my face, and the explosion knocked me down.

When I stood up again, I saw one of the waist gunners was just laid back against the wall of the plane. That was Bill McMaster. I knew right away he was dead. The other waist gunner, Jack Short, had fallen to his knees. At first I thought he might still be alive, but then he fell forward onto his face. That's when I saw a bunch of holes in his helmet. Blood was spurting out of the holes, so I knew he was dead, too.

[6] By 1943 the Luftwaffe was rearming its fighter planes with up to four 20-mm cannons plus two machine guns.

1943

COINCIDING DATES
ON DECEMBER 22, 1943, WHILE ALDRICH FEARED FOR HIS LIFE, ALLIED PROGRESS IN ITALY WAS AT A STANDSTILL. (SEE TIMELINE.)

I don't know why, but just then I remembered it was Jack's birthday, and I remembered him joking in the barracks that morning about how he shouldn't have to go this time because it was his birthday. Another thing I remember was thinking how Jack might still be alive if he and I hadn't traded places back in Moses Lake. I should have been a waist gunner. He should have been down there on the ball turret. We traded places because he was too tall to be a belly gunner, but his name was Jack Short and he died on his twenty-first birthday.

Then I remember looking back at Bill McMaster one last time. He was from Mississippi, one of those "y'all" kind of guys. He was married and had two children, and I thought about the time I met them, when all of us gunners were together in that hotel room back in Walla Walla. I couldn't help thinking about his wife and how worried and afraid she was, not just for Bill, but for all of us.

We were the gunners, and we were buddies. We drank beer together, we'd had some good times, and we really cared about each other. Jack and Bill—they were both too young to die. I was only twenty-two myself. Ever since then I've always said twenty-two must be my lucky number. We were Bomber Crew number twenty-two, I was twenty-two years old, and it was the twenty-second of December.

It was the worst day of my life, but I was alive.

BAILING OUT

I didn't know if I still had time to get out of the plane. There wasn't any fire in the waist section at that point, but I knew we were probably going to explode as soon as the fire on the wing spread to the fuel tank. I had to step around the bodies of the waist gunners to get to the emergency door. I'd just pulled the release handle when all of a sudden I saw the tail gunner, Tony Svoboda, right beside me. I couldn't figure out why he was there. He had his own escape hatch in the tail section, so there was no reason for him to come into the waist to bail out. Maybe he just wanted to see what was going on.

Tony didn't say anything about Jack and Bill, but he had to have walked right past them to get to the emergency door where I was. He must have seen that they were dead. I guess I didn't notice his reaction because everything was happening so fast. All of a sudden he was just there, and we were both standing in the door of the airplane ready to jump out. About the same time I yelled "Go ahead!" at Tony, he was hollering "Go ahead!" to me. So I went!

They tell you to count to ten before you pull the ripcord on your parachute, but I forgot how to count at all just then. Instead, I just pulled it as soon as I could, which turned out to be just long enough for me to clear the airplane.

I was still almost five thousand feet in the air when I saw the plane explode, and I watched what was left after the explosion going down to the ground. The next thing I remember, I was looking up at my parachute. I saw there were holes in it, and I heard something like firecrackers going off. It sounded like the Fourth of July, and I remember thinking that was kind of odd, until I realized it wasn't firecrackers. It was ground fire. Somebody was shooting at me!

I started looking down to see where I was going to land, and the first thing I saw was water. At first I thought I might be over the English Channel. That would mean death, for sure, because you couldn't survive in water as cold as that for very long. Since this was December, the water would be even colder than usual. I wished I'd brought my rubber boat and my life jacket.

As I got closer to the ground, I saw it wasn't the Channel. It looked more like some kind of a canal, so then I figured I had to be somewhere over Holland, or maybe France. I could see a barge on the canal with a whole bunch of people riding on it. I was only about two hundred feet in the air at that point, close enough to hear them cheering for me.[1] I could see they were all waving at me, too. I waved back as I floated by.

 Most Dutch citizens viewed Nazism as ungodly and were either secretly or openly opposed to the German military. The Germans had invaded Holland in 1940 and occupied it for the remainder of the war.

I came down in a meadow, a real nice meadow with short grass. I landed feet-first, then my knees hit the ground, then my hands and face. I got a bloody nose from that. It felt kind of like I'd just jumped off a two-story building. I was sure glad it was such nice, soft grass.

I stood up and looked around. I didn't see anybody at all so I bent down and picked up my parachute. When I looked up again, there was Bill Tracy walking toward me. He was the Martin gunner and the plane's engineer. Right after that, I saw Tony. I think the first thing I said to either of them was, "Jack and Bill are dead."

For the next few minutes the three of us just stood there on the edge of that canal, talking about what to do next. We knew we'd better get out of that meadow—it was too open—so we looked around and saw some woods about fifty feet away. That looked like a good place to hide, so we had just decided to head that way when we saw another guy walking toward us. He was wearing some kind of a uniform.

The man spoke to us in English and asked if we were English. We said, "No, we're Americanisch." Then he told us he was a Dutch policeman and asked if we wanted to get in contact with the Underground.[2] We said we did. The fellow pointed toward the woods and said for us to hide there. "Wait," he said. "I'll go and find somebody from the Underground for you."

Well, Bill, Tony, and I—we figured we had it made then. We all started to relax a little. I took off my helmet.

⭐[2] A secret network of citizens formed to resist an enemy; often established in occupied countries.

10

BETRAYED AND CAPTURED

As soon as the Dutch policeman left us, we walked real fast to get into the woods. There wasn't any snow on the ground—Holland has a coastal climate like Seattle's—so we didn't have to worry about leaving tracks for anybody to follow. When we got to the woods, the first thing I did was bury my parachute. It was white and easy to spot when you're on the ground. I didn't have any tools, so I did the best I could just with my hands. I buried my escape maps, too. They were printed on silk scarves, but all they showed was the outlines of the countries. I didn't think they'd be very helpful.

After that there was nothing for us to do but wait. We didn't have any food with us, and nobody had any cigarettes because we couldn't smoke during a bombing mission. We just stood around and talked. We didn't know if anybody else had got out of the plane alive, and we didn't know what was going to happen when the Underground came to get us. Anybody who flew over Europe during the war knew about the Underground. We'd heard they were a real tough bunch, and if you got taken in by them it didn't mean you were going to have it easy. It was still better than being captured by the Germans, though.

So there we were, the three of us, hiding in the woods, wondering when the Dutch policeman was going to come back for us. It wasn't too long a wait, maybe half an hour at the most. I heard him whistle first, and then he hollered at us to come out. As soon as we stepped out of the trees I saw he was the same guy, all right, but he'd brought about a dozen German soldiers with him. And they all had their rifles up and pointed straight at us.

I just froze where I stood. This young German lieutenant stepped a little closer to me and said, "*Was ist das?*"—"What is that?" He was pointing at the bulge inside my coveralls. All it was, was my leather helmet. When I took it off earlier, I'd folded it up and stuffed it down inside my empty shoulder holster. Well, like a damn fool, I reached for it. The next thing I knew, the fellow had his pistol right up to my nose. I guess he must have thought I was going for my gun. I put my hands back up on my head, and then he reached down inside my coveralls himself. When he pulled out my helmet, he laughed.

After that the Germans checked Bill and Tony to make sure they didn't have any weapons either. Then they loaded all three of us in the back of a truck and drove us to the place where our plane had crashed. Just before we got to the wreckage, they stopped and picked up some more soldiers. Celusnak, the bombardier, was with them. I don't know how he got captured—

maybe it was the same Dutch policeman that found us—but now there were four of us in the truck.

Celusnak told us he saw Jack Bennett, the navigator, bail out of the plane. I guess they pretty much jumped together, just like Tony and I did, but Celusnak didn't find Bennett anywhere on the ground, so he didn't know for sure if he made it. I asked him if he'd seen Dick Dabney. He said he hadn't seen anybody else's parachute except for Jack Bennett's. Based on that, we all assumed Dabney never got out, that he probably went down with the plane.

There wasn't much to look at when we got to the crash site, just some pieces of metal sticking out of the ground and the smell of smoke all around it. I didn't see any bodies or parachutes.

The Germans didn't appear to be too interested in inspecting the wreckage, and they wouldn't let us get out of the truck to look at it either. They tried talking to us, but I couldn't speak German and the other three didn't know it either. One of the soldiers just kept holding up his fingers and pointing at the plane. I gathered they wanted to know how many were in the crew, to see if they should be looking for more prisoners, probably. After a while they gave up—I think it was only about fifteen minutes or so—and then they took us away.[1]

I figured four of our crew were killed that day: the waist gunners, Jack Short and Bill McMaster, for sure, and probably the pilot and copilot, Mangis and Lembcke. I wasn't quite as certain about Dabney. If Dabney didn't bail out in time, that meant five dead. Five out of a crew of ten. We were a real close-knit group of guys. I was sorry. I don't remember feeling anything else; maybe I was in shock. Somehow, I think I just accepted it. I didn't cry.

 Under the provisions of the Geneva Convention, prisoners of war were to be removed promptly from the battle area, given adequate medical care, and housed and fed no worse than garrison troops of the capturing power.

PRISONER OF WAR

With the four of us riding in the back of the truck, the Germans drove to a little town not far from Amsterdam. I don't remember the name of the town; what I mainly remember is the jail. It was just an ordinary small-town jail, not anything that was built especially for housing prisoners of war. This jail had one window that looked out on a village square. I could see a few cows and some farmers gathered out there, and I heard them shouting about something. I didn't understand German, but it sounded like they might have been arguing about the price of cattle. They were definitely buying and selling something, so I just assumed it had to do with the cows.

The soldiers put the three sergeant gunners—Bill, Tony, and me—all in the same cell. I don't know where they took Celusnak. He was a commissioned officer so, according to the rules of the

Geneva Convention, he had to be housed separately from non-commissioned officers.

There were cots for us in the jail cell, but I had such a bad headache I couldn't sleep at all that night. Worst headache I ever had in my whole life. I think what caused it was I'd had a cold, and then, with the sudden change in air pressure when the plane was losing altitude, my ears were all stopped up. After I bailed out, right before I touched the ground, I heard something like a pop inside my head, and I felt something running out of my right ear. I didn't find out what happened until years later when I was examined by a doctor. He told me my right eardrum had been broken.

The next morning, the Germans took us to a train depot. While we were waiting to board, a group of Dutch civilians came up and tried to talk to us, but the Germans wouldn't let them. Finally, one of the men bought a bottle of lemon pop and handed it to me. I thought that was pretty nice, but the guard wouldn't let me have it. *"Nicht! Nicht! Nicht!"* he said.

The Germans kept us under heavy guard. There were way more guards than I thought they needed for just the three of us. So far as I could tell, we were the only prisoners of war on that train, and everyone else appeared to be civilians. As it turned out, the train stopped to pick up more prisoners along the way. By the time we got to Amsterdam, there must have been twenty-five or more prisoners of war on board.[1] Some were British; most were Americans. I talked to some of them. It was just small talk—about girls, probably—to pass the time.

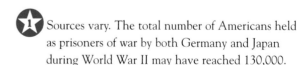 Sources vary. The total number of Americans held as prisoners of war by both Germany and Japan during World War II may have reached 130,000.

When we got to Amsterdam, they put us on a truck and drove us to another jail. Again, it was the three of us—Bill, Tony, and I—all in the same cell. The guards made us take off our flight suits, the long johns with the heat coils in them, so all I had left was my underwear and coveralls. I'm not sure why the Germans wouldn't let us keep our flight suits on, unless maybe they wanted to use them for their own fliers.

There was no toilet in the cell. You had to rattle the bars if you had to go to the latrine. So, one time I banged on the bars, and when I got to the latrine I ran into our first navigator, Faragasso. He was the one we had before he got transferred to another crew, back when we were all in St. Louis for the pilot's first instrument test. We were sure surprised to see each other! I talked with him for a little while, but the guard wouldn't let me stay long enough to hear his shot-down story. I never saw him again after that.

We were in that jail in Amsterdam for three days altogether. I did realize when it was Christmas Eve, but I don't recall that causing me any extra sadness. It was my second Christmas away from home, so I don't think that part of it bothered me too much. I remember they gave us potato salad and wieners for dinner on Christmas Day.

The day after Christmas, the Germans took us from Amsterdam to Frankfurt [Frankfurt am Main, Germany] by train. There were about thirty of us, all prisoners of war, in the train car; I don't know how many cars there were altogether. It was what they called a day coach. I remember everybody sitting in rows on these wooden bench-type seats. Some of the guys tried to sleep, but we were pretty crowded together and those benches weren't too comfortable.

Several times during the trip the train had to stop because of a bombing raid. I never saw any of the formations overhead, but I knew they had to be American because it was during the day.[2] Everybody had to hurry to get off the train and take shelter wherever we could. One time the guards took us down into the basement of a railroad station, and we all waited there together until they decided the bombers were gone and it was safe to come out and get back on the train.

Somewhere along the line—just inside the German border, I think it was—the guards started going down the aisle, pulling down the shades on all the windows. That surprised me, but they told us they had to do that so the German civilians wouldn't see us. Cologne had been just flattened by our bombs, they said, and the civilians were really mad at us—the Americans and the British.[3] I didn't really believe it until we got to Frankfurt. After that, I thought it probably was a good thing the guards pulled the shades.

Somewhere around Cologne, the train stopped again. That time it was to let some gals from the German Red Cross get on.[4] They had a big kettle full of barley soup, and they went down the aisle and gave us each a bowl. It tasted pretty good, but shortly after that we all got diarrhea. We thought it must have been from the soup.

When we got to Frankfurt, we had to get off the train and wait for a trolley to take us to another prison. A mob of civilians began to gather around us. There must have been at least a hundred of

[2] From June 1943 through January 1944, the British RAF (Royal Air Force) bombed German targets at the average rate of 183 sorties per night while the U.S. Eighth Air Force carried out day bombings averaging 120 sorties per day. (A "sortie" is one mission by one airplane.)

[3] Because of its location just 40 miles (64 kilometers) east of the Dutch border and its railroad marshaling yards, the cathedral city of Cologne was the first German city targeted for a large-scale British attack. In May 1942 more than a thousand planes dropped 1,455 tons (about 1,300 metric tons) of bombs in one night. The city continued to be pounded by British and American bombers for the duration of the war.

[4] The original purpose of the Red Cross was to provide medical care for wounded soldiers. Under the Geneva Convention its purpose was extended to include humane treatment for prisoners of war. The "gals" mentioned here were undoubtedly volunteers, as are the majority of workers in this international organization.

them, mostly men—older-looking men, I thought—and they were really riled up. They started spitting at us and shouting, *"Schweinhund! Schweinhund!"*—"dirty dog." Then I noticed a lot of them had rocks and bottles, and it looked like they were going to throw them at us. I couldn't really blame them for being mad. They knew we were some of the bombers who were destroying their homes.[5]

The only protection we had was one German guard. He was really worried, too, or at least he seemed to be by the look on his face. He shouted back at them, *"Raus! Raus!"*—"Get out"—and he pointed his gun at them. I suppose they knew he couldn't disperse that big a mob all by himself, so they just kept shouting and spitting. I was pretty scared there for a while, but somehow the guard managed to keep the crowd far enough away from us until the trolley came. When it did, we all got on it right quick, including the guard.

5 Although American bombing raids targeted military and factory facilities, some bombs missed their mark and hit nonmilitary areas. In all, Allied bombs killed approximately 600,000 German civilians. As a result, irate civilians often roughed up crews that bailed out of disabled planes before turning them over to the military.

1943

COINCIDING DATES

FROM DECEMBER 22–27, 1943, WHILE ALDRICH WAS IN PRISON, THE ALLIES WERE PREPARING TO INVADE GERMAN-OCCUPIED FRANCE AND PRESIDENT ROOSEVELT NAMED GENERAL DWIGHT D. EISENHOWER AS COMMANDER. (SEE TIMELINE.)

INTERROGATION BY THE NAZIS

It wasn't a very long ride, so I think we were still somewhere in or around Frankfurt when the guards told us to get off the trolley in front of this big building. They called it the *Dulagluft*.[1] I couldn't tell if it had been converted from something else or if it was built specifically to house prisoners of war. When I was there it was definitely a prison. The Germans put me in a cell by myself. I didn't know where they were taking Bill and Tony, but I assumed they each got their own cells, too. This was the first time we'd been separated since we got captured.

My cell was very small, I'd say about eight feet by eight feet. The room was clean, but there was nothing in it except a table and chair and a cot with a sheet on it. No blankets. There was a single lightbulb on the ceiling, but no heat. No toilet, either. Once again, I had to pound on the door if I wanted a guard to come and take me to the latrine. I did have one window, but it was too high for me to see anything out of.

[1] A transit camp at Oberursel, near Frankfurt am Main, through which the Luftwaffe passed captured aircrew and interrogated them.

The uncertainty was the worst part of being there. For all I knew, the Germans were planning to torture or shoot me. I just didn't know. And I was always scared when I heard bombers coming over the city. It sounded like the bombs were exploding right outside my window. What I heard was actually AA [antiaircraft] fire, but I didn't know that while I was in solitary confinement. It wasn't until later, when I got a chance to talk to other prisoners, that one of them told me the Germans had an antiaircraft gun right below my window. I never saw it myself, but it must have been a big one.

I got one slice of bread a day and water, or some ersatz tea. I don't know what it was, really. It didn't taste like tea, and it wasn't hot enough. Sometimes the bread had a sweet spread on it. I expected the bread to be stale, but it actually tasted fresh. The texture of it was more like cake than bread. The slice I got every day was about an inch thick and about the size of a saucer, except it was oval-shaped. It was so good. I've never tasted anything like it before or since. I've always dreamed of having another slice of that black bread with a big slice of Swiss cheese on it.

Once a day the guards came to take me to somebody's office for interrogation. It was never the same guy doing the interrogating, but the sessions usually lasted about the same amount of time, about a half hour each. The Air Force never gave me any instructions on what to do or say if I was captured. I knew we weren't supposed to say anything except name, rank, and serial number. Usually the interrogator would just make a statement, and I'd shrug. I don't know what I said.

As near as I could tell, the only purpose of the interrogations was to confirm what they already knew. They knew I'd been trained in Walla Walla, how many were in my crew, and everywhere we'd been, including Moses Lake and St. Louis. Their spies were very good. I think the Germans must have been hoping one of us might be somebody important. They sure seemed to know an ordinary sergeant gunner like me wasn't anybody who could tell them anything they didn't already know.

It was better to be interrogated than to be in that cell, in solitary confinement. It was mostly dark, so I just slept most of the time, except for when the guards woke me up for meals or more interrogation. It wasn't that I was so mentally or physically exhausted at that point; I think the reason I slept so much was boredom.

I remember dreaming a lot, mainly about being home and doing things with my parents. That helped to pass the time. When I was awake I just kept imagining what was going to happen next. I didn't know what to expect. I didn't know how long the Germans were going to keep me there, or if maybe they were going to kill me. As it turned out, I was never tortured or physically abused in any way, other than having to stay in solitary confinement.

There was this one German colonel. They took me into his office and left me alone with him. He was sitting behind a desk when I came in, and I noticed he had on a different kind of uniform. I'm sure he was SS.[2] Pretty soon he looked up at me, and then he just started rattling off all the facts about our crew, in English. He knew all our names and every detail. I figured he might have even seen the picture of us that was in *The Spokesman Review*

⭐**2** The SS, short for *Schutzstaffel* (protection squad), were uniformed Nazi soldiers known for their bravery and fierce loyalty and obedience to Hitler, their Führer (leader). They wore black uniforms and boots and caps upon which they pinned a small metal skull.

[a Spokane, Washington, newspaper]. He never once asked me a question; he just told me everything he already knew.

There was something different about his attitude. He was more cheerful, more relaxed than the other interrogators I'd had, and he spoke real soft. He even offered me a cigarette. "You want a Chesterfield?" he said. My brand was Camels, but I took it from him. He gave me a wooden match to light it with, and I smoked it right there in his office. I thought it might signify the last time I was going to be interrogated. And it did.

I wasn't sure what day it was when they took me out of solitary confinement. That one lightbulb was on all the time, so it was hard to tell if it was day or night. I didn't try to make a system of keeping time, probably because I slept so much. I thought I was there for two weeks, but after I got out I found out it was only a week. It sure seemed longer than that.

The guards took me out of the prison building and put me on another train. This time it was a boxcar, like the kind for moving cattle. Bill and Tony were there, too, so the three of us were back together again, all in the same boxcar with about thirty other prisoners of war. It was so crowded you couldn't lie down, and there wasn't any toilet so we just had to designate a corner for everybody to go. There wasn't much any of us could do but talk to each other. Mostly we traded shot-down stories. Some of it, I'm sure, was just a lot of b.s.

That train ride lasted about a week. We had to stop a lot so they could let other higher priority trains go by, and sometimes we were allowed to get out of the boxcar while we waited. The

COINCIDING DATES

DURING ALDRICH'S DAYS AT DULAGLUFT, LATE DECEMBER 1943 TO EARLY 1944, THE GERMANS WERE IMPROVING THEIR DEFENSES ALONG THE FRENCH COASTLINE IN ANTICIPATION OF AN ALLIED INVASION. (SEE TIMELINE.)

weather was pretty cold, around thirty degrees it felt like, and there was a lot of snow on the ground. I still wasn't sure what day it was, but I knew it had to be some time in January.

Sometimes, while we were standing outside during a stop, we'd see an American P-47 coming in for a strafing run[3] and then we'd run for cover. The guards, the prisoners, everybody had to hurry and get down behind a building, trees, shrubs—whatever we could find.

The Germans were really scared of those strafing runs. So were we, but I didn't realize I was in that much danger until the time I saw this German soldier on a bicycle. I never saw anybody jump off a bicycle as fast as he did when the American fighters were coming. First he tried to shove the bike into some bushes. I think he was trying to hide it so nobody would steal it. I could see he wasn't having much luck with that idea, and then I saw him look up at the sky. Then he just dropped the bike on the ground and took off running away from the train tracks as fast as he could go.

When the fighters came over, it looked to me like they were only about two hundred feet above the ground, strafing the train and everything around it. It was pretty scary to be shot at that way, but I can't say it bothered me knowing the bullets were coming from my own countrymen. They were doing what they had to do; they couldn't have known they might be killing American prisoners of war.

I never saw antiaircraft fire any of the times the fighters were strafing. I don't know why. Maybe the Germans didn't have any AA guns in that area, or, just as likely, they might have been under orders to save their ammunition for the bombers.

3 To strafe means to fire at close range, especially with machine guns from low-flying aircraft. As the flying range of American fighter planes increased, so did the frequency and intensity of these strafing runs.

STALAG 17

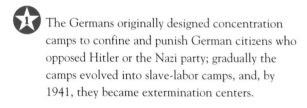

The Germans originally designed concentration camps to confine and punish German citizens who opposed Hitler or the Nazi party; gradually the camps evolved into slave-labor camps, and, by 1941, they became extermination centers.

Although the largest number of those killed by the Nazis were Jews (six million), other victims included Soviet prisoners of war, Gypsies, the handicapped, homosexuals, pacifists, political prisoners, non-Jewish eastern Europeans, intellectuals, criminals, and even other Nazis.

Auschwitz was a gigantic complex of concentration and slave-labor camps in Poland in which millions were killed, tortured, and/or starved.

The last stop was in Austria, near a little town called Krems, about thirty miles outside of Vienna. When we got off the train and all the boxcars were unloaded at once, I could see there were about two hundred of us. I'd guess twenty-five were British and the rest were Americans.

I'd heard the term "concentration camp" and I knew that was where the Germans were sending the Jews, but I thought that was just another name for a prisoner-of-war camp.[1] I had no idea there was so much difference between the two.

At that time we didn't really know what kind of man Hitler was. We thought he was crazy, but we didn't know the Nazis were killing Jews in concentration camps by the thousands every day.[2] I didn't hear about Auschwitz[3] or any of those kinds of places until a long time afterwards.

The first thing we had to do after we got off the train was march up a hill. Then the guards took us into a building and shaved off all our hair. After that, we had to take off all our clothes and then they ran us through a cold-water shower. That was to delouse us, I guess. They didn't give us any towels to dry off with, so we had to just stand there wet and naked for a long time.

Everybody was wondering what was going to happen next; nobody knew what to expect. I would have been a lot more scared than I was if I had known what the Germans were doing to the Jews.[4] I felt helpless as hell, but I guess I thought there was safety in numbers. I had no idea how wrong I was.

I finally found a wet towel and tried to dry myself off a little with that. It was so cold and damp in the shower building, I couldn't stop shivering. Pretty soon I couldn't talk anymore because my teeth were chattering. Finally the guards gave us our clothes—the same ones we came in with—and we had to march back down the hill and about another two miles to the prison camp. I think it was around five o'clock in the afternoon. It was snowing; the temperature had to have been somewhere in the teens. My feet got so cold I thought they were going to drop off.

Tony, Bill, and I were still together when we marched into the prison camp. The guards took us into a wooden barracks building about the size of a small gymnasium. They let us pick our own bunk from any that were empty. There weren't that many empty ones. The bunk beds were stacked three tiers high, but nobody slept on the top ones. Those were just for storage.

There was no heat in the barracks at all, except for body heat. The Germans gave us each two blankets, which was what we were supposed to get according to the rules of the Geneva Convention.

 After being forced to undress as if for bathing, thousands at Auschwitz were brought into a "shower room," locked inside, and then gassed. Afterward, their bodies were burned. Also at Auschwitz, a German doctor, Josef Mengele, carried out torturous experiments on prisoners. Details of the killing and mistreatment of Jews at Auschwitz did not reach Allied capitals until the summer of 1944, a full two years after the killings had begun.

Mug shots of Dale Aldrich after he arrived at Stalag 17 in January 1944

 Stalag is a contraction of the German word *Stammlager*, meaning prison for "common stock," or servicemen below officer rank. Although the Germans designated separate camps for commissioned officers, all prison camps for captured airmen were called "Stalags."

 Total number of Allied prisoners, excluding Soviets, held by Germany during World War II: approximately 1.73 million, of which it is estimated 765,000 were French; 550,000 Italian; 200,000 British; 125,000 Yugoslav; 90,000 American. (Most of the 90 POW camps were in Germany; Stalag 17 was one of 11 in Austria.)

Actually, it was just one blanket cut in half—dirty, old, frayed around the edges. It wasn't wool; some kind of cotton, I think. It didn't look like it was ever a German army blanket because it had some kind of design on the material. I'd guess it was either donated or taken from a civilian household.

The guys in the barracks shared their food with us. All they had was some leftover soup, and I thought it was carrot soup from the looks of it. That was all right because I like carrots, but then I found out it wasn't carrots. It was rutabagas. I didn't like rutabagas, but the soup was so tasteless with no salt, it didn't matter. And, by that time I was hungry enough to eat anything.

After we ate and got settled in a little bit, we started to talk and get acquainted with the guys who were there. There might have been a few other ranks of noncommissioned officers, but everybody I met was a sergeant gunner like me. They told me what day it was—that's when I found out it was the eighth of January—and we traded stories. All the shot-down stories I heard sounded pretty much like mine.

They told us that the name of the camp was Stalag 17,[5] and that we were in Section B of the American Compound. I think there were about four thousand Americans altogether. There were men of other nationalities, too—British, French, Italian, Russian—all of them prisoners of war just like us. I never knew for sure how many there were because the Germans kept all the nationalities separate from each other.[6] They had their own compounds, and we weren't allowed to go near them.

The main entrance to Stalag 17. Here prisoners are returning to the camp from a delousing procedure.

The guards piled empty food cans along the double fence surrounding the American Compound at Stalag 17 so anybody trying to escape would make noise.

The wooden barracks at Stalag 17 were unheated and bug infested.

A fenced corridor separated the A and B sections of the American Compound.

The A and B sections of the American Compound were each about the size of a city block—big enough to play baseball at one end, anyway. There was a kind of a narrow street—more like a corridor, really—separating the two sections. You could walk back and forth between them if you wanted to, but only in the daytime.

There was a ten-foot-high double fence of barbed wire going around both sections of the American Compound, and they had a single warning wire twenty feet inside that. The warning wire wasn't electric; it was just there to tell you if you got between it and the double fence you'd be shot.

There were about three hundred Americans in the barracks I got assigned to; the building was divided in half with 150 prisoners and one guard at each end. I think that was how all the barracks were organized, or at least they were in our compound. In the whole camp, I'd say there were maybe thirty buildings just like it.

We had what we called a "barracks chief." I don't know, but he was probably the guy who'd been in the building the longest, and all the barracks chiefs had their own buddies. These prisoners let us in on some of the rules of the camp: the most forbidden thing for us to have was a weapon, and the only thing anybody could get shot for was trying to escape, or for going outside after dark. They told us most of the guards weren't too bad, but there were a couple who'd been to the Russian front.[7] Everybody said these guards were really rough and to stay out of their way as much as you could.

 Beginning in June 1941, Germany invaded Soviet territory in eastern Europe; German troops serving on the Russian front were ill-equipped and faced the harsh Russian winters with inadequate food, clothing, and supplies.

COINCIDING DATES

IN JANUARY 1944, AS ALDRICH LEARNED THE ROPES AT STALAG 17, THE ALLIES WERE PLANNING A TWO-PRONGED OFFENSIVE TOWARD ROME THROUGH MONTE CASSINO AND ANZIO. (SEE TIMELINE.)

447 DAYS

At Stalag 17, every day began with a whistle. It sounded just like a basketball referee's, except it was at seven in the morning, and it meant you were supposed to fall out for *Appell*—German for roll call. We had two roll calls every day—that one in the morning and then another at 6 P.M. You had to go outside the barracks and line up by fives so the guards could count you.

We always had the same guard doing the counting for our barracks. If he didn't come up with the number of prisoners he was supposed to have, he'd call for some more guards, and they'd all go in and search the barracks. Then they'd come back out and just keep counting us until they got the right number. That could take anywhere from fifteen minutes to half an hour. In the winter, it seemed like forever.

After the morning roll call we could go back inside, and then some of the guys would bring in this big wooden tub full of hot

Appell—*roll call*

On Red Cross Parcel Day prisoners hurry back to their barracks to unpack their parcels, which usually included food, coffee, and cigarettes.

Prisoners in the American Compound haul a large wooden tub of hot water to their barracks.

water. I'd guess it to be about a forty- or fifty-gallon tub; I know it took two guys to carry it. We used that to make our coffee in the morning. There was no breakfast, other than that hot water for coffee.

At noon, they would bring in the same tub filled with rutabaga soup. There were maggots in the soup, and I knew it, but I'd just go over to a dark corner to eat so I couldn't see them. Sometimes, instead of soup, the tub would be filled with potatoes cooked in their jackets, and there were usually some little pieces of black bread to go with the soup or the potatoes. It was the same kind of bread I got when I was in solitary in Frankfurt, only not quite as fresh. Sometimes, to go on the bread, the Germans would give us this stuff that looked and tasted kind of like honey, but not as sweet. We called it "Jerry jam." What it was, I think, was the left-overs from their smashed sugar beets.

The only other food we had was whatever we got in our Red Cross parcels.[1] Those came once a week. Parcel Day at Stalag 17 was a really big deal. To us, it was kind of like payday—the only day we really looked forward to. When we were extra hungry, we'd just sit around the barracks and count the hours until Parcel Day.

Bill and Tony and I all arrived at Stalag 17 at the same time, but we didn't stay together much after we got there. Their bunks weren't very close to mine, and they each found a buddy from their hometown to combine with. A "combine" was what we called a group of guys that shared things like food from Red Cross parcels. You could have any number in a combine, but usually it was just two. My first combine buddy was a farm boy from Minnesota. He

⭐[1] The POWs were preoccupied with food, and for most of the war the Red Cross had been able to get food and comfort parcels to the British and American POWs regularly.

had a blonde crew cut, and he was about the same size and age as me. I think his name was Van Dyke; I don't remember much else about him. We were only together for about three months, and it seemed like all he and I ever talked about was food and how long it was going to be before we got some more.

Red Cross Parcel Day was always on Friday, usually sometime in the morning. Somebody would holler out, "They're here!" and then we'd all run out of the barracks and down to another building. It might have been the camp kitchen, but I'm not sure. All I ever saw of it was one big room with a bunch of tables, all loaded with cardboard boxes. As soon as you got into the room you'd pick one of those tables and line up in front of it, single file.

The lids on all the big boxes there were already opened, and inside each of those were four individual parcels, one for each prisoner. There was at least one guard behind every table, but he wouldn't hand you a parcel until he'd run his bayonet through all the cans of food. That was so we couldn't hoard any for escape supplies.

The food in a Red Cross parcel was about the same every week. There was always one can of instant coffee, another can with powdered milk, and a six-ounce package of cubed sugar. Plus, you usually got a half pound of cheddar cheese, a can of salmon, and a little package of C-ration-type[2] crackers. And one semisweet chocolate bar. You could eat it all at once if you wanted to, but that was all you got for a whole week. I always tried to ration it out to myself so I wouldn't run out before the next Parcel Day.

That first year, in 1944, we got one Red Cross parcel per prisoner every Friday. Later, it was one parcel for five men to share. Then it varied.[3] It was just a question of how many men would have to divide one. The guards told us it was because our bombers were destroying the train routes the parcels came in on. That might have been true, but we all suspected the Germans were really starting to have trouble with their own supply lines at that point during the war.[4] We figured they were probably keeping some of our parcels for themselves.

Once in a while some Red Cross representatives would come in to inspect the conditions in the prison camp. We really liked that because whenever the Red Cross came, the Germans would give us more food than usual. We were supposed to be fed the same as the guards, in theory. I never saw what the guards ate, but I'm pretty sure they got more than we did, except when the Red Cross was there.

If it hadn't been for those Red Cross food parcels, I wouldn't be here today. I'd have just starved to death the way the Russians did. Their government never signed the rules of the Geneva Convention, so Russian prisoners of war didn't receive any Red Cross parcels at all. Every day I saw them go past our building carrying dead Russians wrapped in paper. They were dying of starvation.

Even more Russians died in the winter—from pneumonia, probably. I felt bad for those guys. We would have helped them if we could, but the guards kept us from going anywhere near their

 The supply of Red Cross parcels began to dry up in late 1944 after Heinrich Himmler took command of the German Replacement Army and POW camps.

 Allied air attacks on German transportation continued throughout 1944 and brought rail traffic almost to a standstill by 1945.

By the spring of 1944, the Germans had captured more than five million Soviet soldiers. Only about one out of five survived the brutal treatment of the Germans. Russian POWs were subjected to forced labor, deliberate starvation, and the denial of even the most primitive medical help.

 By the war's end, as many as 11 million people died in this Holocaust. German policy in this respect was dictated by Nazi racial myth, which held that Anglo-Saxons (British and other Caucasians of western European ancestry) were Aryans—therefore worthy of respect—while Slavs (Russians, Poles, eastern Europeans) were lesser humans, barely superior to cattle.

compound. There was nothing we could do but watch the bodies go by.[5] [6]

Compared to the Russians', my experience as a prisoner of war wasn't that bad. Still, it's amazing nobody I knew ever got sick. I never even caught a cold the whole time I was there. I never had to work, either, and I don't know of any other Americans who did. But all the Americans were officers. Some of the other nationalities at Stalag 17 were not officers, so they could be taken outside the prison camp to work.

Actually, it would have been better to work. It would have given me something to do to ease the boredom. Also, the prisoners who got to work outside the camp always got more food. The ones who worked on farms had the best deal of all. They could get eggs and vegetables and other kinds of things by trading with the farmers.

American cigarettes were the medium of exchange. You usually traded them for extra food, but you could get other things if you had the right contacts. The idea was to make friends with the guards and get them to look the other way while you traded with prisoners in other parts of the prison camp. In the evening, prisoners from different compounds would meet at the fences between the compounds. Very few of us had direct access to the people who were out trading at the fences because they had to bribe the guards, and all that had to be kept pretty hush-hush.

There were always five packs of cigarettes—twenty in each pack—in every Red Cross parcel, plus you could get one "cigarette parcel" a month from home. My family knew I was missing in action by January [1944]—they were notified by the Air Corps—but it was all the way into April before the Red Cross told them I was alive and in a prison camp. After that, Mom started sending me cigarettes.

A cigarette parcel could contain up to six cartons. There were ten packs in a carton; they cost five cents a pack. My mother sent the money directly to Camel, and then Camel sent a parcel to me every month. I smoked a lot while I was in the prison camp, about two packs a day. Everybody did. Cigarettes helped ease the constant hunger. Of course, that was before anybody knew how bad for you they were.

Besides the one cigarette parcel a month, about every six weeks we could receive a small personal package from home. My mother kept those coming on a pretty regular basis, but the only one I really remember was the one that had a pair of white flannel pajamas. They were really nice, but they were black after the first night I slept in them because I was so dirty. I wore them anyway every night after that until they wore out. The fabric just fell apart; they wouldn't stay on me anymore. I felt real bad when I finally had to throw away those pajamas. They sure felt good.

The French and Italian prisoners had wine. I don't know if they got it from trading with the civilians or if it came in their packages from home. Most likely, they got it from the German guards. Some guards could be bribed, usually with cigarettes, but I never knew which ones. Everything like that was kind of a secret, and you never told what guard you bribed or what your sources were.

I never saw any alcohol to speak of in the American Compound. Oh, sometimes there'd be boxes of raisins in our Red Cross parcels, and some of the guys figured out they could ferment the raisins in tin cans and make a kind of a wine out of that. "Raisin jack," we called it. I don't know what raisin jack tasted like because I never cared to try any. You could make vodka out of the potatoes, too, but I didn't drink any of that either. In fact, I never had any alcohol at all the whole time I was in the prison camp.

The Red Cross also sent American-made clothes for us to wear. In the spring and summer we had khaki pants and shirts made out of cotton; for fall and winter we wore our ODs. That means olive drab. Those were wool. And we all had one long wool GI overcoat. We slept in those. We really needed them in the winter, too, because there was never any heat in the barracks. It was so cold that first winter, my combine buddy and I even slept together in the same bunk just so we could stay warm enough to sleep. That didn't bother me at all. He always curled himself up against my back, and I liked that because my back hurt when it got cold.

The barracks were all wired for electricity, but it was not usually turned on. I guess it was too expensive for the Germans to keep the electricity on. I know the guards didn't want us using it to heat water. All we had to wash with was cold water in this big, long trough, and the only way we could keep it from freezing in the winter was to leave it running all the time.

If you can imagine shaving with ice-cold water, some of the guys grew beards because of that. One man had a long red beard all the way down his chest. He was brokenhearted when the guards said he had to shave it off. It really was a beautiful beard, and everybody felt sorry for him when he had to shave it. I don't know why the Germans did that. Maybe they thought he was going to attract lice; maybe it was just to show us who was in charge.

About every three months, we had to be deloused. The Germans gave us that same shower treatment we got when we first came into the prison camp, and then they gassed our clothes to kill the lice. We had bedbugs, too. I had bites and rashes from them all over my body most of the time.

We knew where the bedbugs were at night—they were in our beds—but we didn't know where they went during the daytime. Finally, somebody noticed there were a lot of empty nail holes all over the barracks. We found out that if you poked a nail into one of those empty nail holes, when you pulled it back out again, the nail would be covered with blood—your blood. So that's how we knew where the bedbugs were all day. It gave us something to do. We had all the time in the world to sit around and think of stuff like that.

Boredom wasn't as bad as hunger, but it was right up there with the worst part of being in a prisoner-of-war camp. The Germans wouldn't let us get any books or magazines from the Red Cross or from home. I suppose that was because they would have wanted to censor everything, and they didn't have enough interpreters to do that in a camp the size of Stalag 17. The only newspaper we could have was a German one—I think it was called the *Berebacher*[7] or something like that. It was fairly useless for actual news, even after I got so I could read it. I'd have given anything for a *Reader's Digest*, any month.

There was only one latrine building for the whole American Compound at Stalag 17. Once a week the guards brought in a "honey wagon" to pump out the sewage.

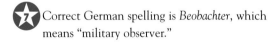 Correct German spelling is *Beobachter*, which means "military observer."

We could write letters—the Germans gave us special forms to write on—but they only allowed you to send four of those a month. I generally split mine up between my mother and Jackie.

Jackie had been writing to me all along, ever since I graduated from Air College. I got about two letters a month from her while I was in the prison camp, and I really looked forward to them. I never told Jackie I loved her when I was in St. Louis, and we'd never talked about getting married. But I could tell that was what she had in mind because in a couple of her letters she told me she was filling up her hope chest.

My hometown girlfriend never did write to me when I was in prison. That was no surprise; I'd stopped getting letters from her shortly before I left for England. I had an idea she'd married somebody else about halfway through the time I was in the prison camp. I kind of expected that, too, but I didn't know for sure. Mom wasn't too crazy about her, so she never said anything. I knew better than to ask.

My mother was the only one who wrote to me from home. That was all right because she told me everything there was to know about what she and Dad and Ted and my sisters were doing, plus the news from around town.

I was surprised when Mom said my wallet never showed up. I really trusted that ground-crew chief back at Horham when I asked him to mail it to my folks if I got shot down. He promised he would, and I believed him. I don't know why he didn't, unless maybe something happened to him, too.

Besides reading and writing letters, we played a lot of cards in the barracks. That helped pass the time. Poker was pretty popular—the stakes were cigarettes—and I learned to play bridge the first winter I was there.

In the spring and summer, the Red Cross sent us horseshoes and some balls and bats. We had a regular softball league going that first summer. We even had some professional and semipro baseball players who'd volunteered or got drafted and then got shot down like the rest of us.[8] It was a lot of fun to watch them play ball. Everybody bet on the games. The stakes were always cigarettes.

I usually won more than I lost; I used my winnings to buy or trade for more food. Once in a while the Red Cross would make a mistake, and you'd get a can of tuna fish in your food parcel instead of the usual salmon. That was worth money, too. You could sell a can of tuna for a lot of cigarettes.

Some of the prisoners bought or traded for crystal sets and made radios. We could get the BBC—British Broadcasting Company—with those, so we usually knew what was going on in the war.

Every now and then the Germans would turn on the electricity in the barracks. The lights would just come on all of a sudden, and then they'd switch it off again after a while. That didn't happen very often, so everybody made their own "candles." You'd take an empty coffee can and put some margarine in it. Then you'd stick a little piece of twisted cloth in the margarine and light it. It worked all right as a candle or a lamp, but it gave off a lot of real

8 More than 4,000 of the 5,700 players in the major and minor leagues went into the service, including baseball greats Joe DiMaggio and Ted Williams.

thick black smoke. Between that and the cigarettes, I'm pretty sure that's when I started to get emphysema.

We also had these little homemade stoves for cooking. You'd take the biggest can you had, which was the one our powdered milk came in—it was about the size of a ten-ounce coffee can. Then you punched a few holes in the side of the can and tore up little pieces of cardboard from the Red Cross packages and put them down inside. That was the fuel. Then you'd put another can on top of the lid of the first can, filled with whatever it was you wanted to heat. That was how we heated our water for coffee or whatever else we wanted warmed.

There were always plenty of matches around, but the Germans didn't like us to have those stoves. They'd take them away from us if they found them, so we always had to hide them. Anything you didn't want the guards to see, you'd stuff under your blankets. They didn't try too hard to find anything that was out of sight, unless they thought you had a radio. I wasn't one of the ones who had a radio, so all I ever had to hide was my stove. The punishment for breaking a prison-camp rule was solitary confinement, but I never got caught for anything that serious. Neither did anybody I knew.

Sometimes a whole bunch of guards would come tearing through the barracks searching for somebody. It could have been for any reason at all, but usually a big search like that only happened if they thought a prisoner had escaped. It was almost impossible to find anybody that way, though, because it was so easy for us to elude a search. Guys would just keep shifting bunks, kind of like a shell game, until the guards would finally give up and leave us alone. We always tried to protect each other that way, even if we didn't know who it was they were after or why.

It wasn't anything like *Hogan's Heroes*.[9] I've seen a few of those shows. I wouldn't say it's painful for me to watch; I just don't find them very realistic. The only thing we did have at Stalag 17 that was the same as in *Hogan's Heroes* was a German guard named Schultz. Our Schultz was a corporal instead of a sergeant like the one on TV, but he was the main guard for our end of the building.

Schultz wasn't any bumbling idiot like the one on *Hogan's Heroes*, either. He took his job very seriously. He would come in and search under our beds and everywhere else for radios and weapons. He never found any, so far as I know. I think he would have just taken them away from us if he had.

Corporal Schultz wasn't too bad of a guy. He probably overlooked a lot of things in our favor, but he wasn't the only guard who could inspect our barracks. All the guards had to be pretty careful because the Germans had a whole network of spies in the camp. If any of the guards showed too much inclination to be nice to us, they could have been shot for treason.

Most of the guards were Austrian, except for Schultz. He was German, but he spoke English really well. I asked him why, and he said it was because he'd gone to high school in Chicago. He even told me how he happened to be at Stalag 17. He said, "I went home from school to visit my parents in Germany. About that time the war started and I got drafted." Schultz said he thought the only rea-

 **9** A television comedy series set in a fictitious World War II German prisoner-of-war camp.

son they made him a guard was because he learned to speak English in America. He also told me he was glad he got assigned to prison-camp duty instead of combat.

Sometimes Schultz would come into the barracks and just visit with us for a few minutes. I think he liked practicing his English. He'd also learned to like coffee when he was in the States, but coffee was too scarce in Germany during the war so he drank ours.

One time somebody dropped some "brown bombers" in the cup before they handed it to him. That was what we called laxatives—those came in our Red Cross parcels, too. We didn't see Schultz at all for about three days after that, and when he did come back he looked pretty weak. We thought it was a good joke on old Schultz, but I don't think he ever found out what happened. He never said anything about it, and he kept coming in for coffee.

Another time, Schultz came into our barracks to do an inspection, and he had to bend over real low to look under somebody's bed. Well, somebody else sneaked up behind him and stole his bayonet—took it right off his rifle while he was still bending over. Pretty soon he noticed it was gone, and that really gave him a scare. He started carrying on about what was going to happen to him if he didn't get his bayonet back, how he was probably going to be shot or get sent to the Russian front. The poor guy was so afraid, I thought he was going to cry. Everybody felt sorry for him, so finally the man who took the bayonet gave it back.

And then there was the time I remember Schultz coming in to get us for roll call. One guy on one of the top bunks wouldn't get

COINCIDING DATES

DURING ALDRICH'S 447 DAYS AT STALAG 17, JANUARY 1944 TO APRIL 1945, THE ALLIES GAINED AIR SUPERIORITY OVER THE GERMANS, MOUNTED A MASSIVE GROUND INVASION, AND ADVANCED INTO GERMANY. MEANWHILE, IN THE PACIFIC THE ALLIES EXPERIENCED BOTH SUCCESSES AND FAILURES. (SEE TIMELINE.)

out of bed. Schultz yelled at him to get up. When that didn't work, he started poking his bayonet up under the guy's bed. Everybody was laughing by that time, but Schultz didn't think it was funny at all. He was just jamming his bayonet into that bed as hard as he could. I don't think I've ever laughed as hard as I did then, but I'm not sure why.

There really wasn't very much to laugh about at Stalag 17. Being a prisoner of war was scary and uncomfortable most of the time, and it was just hard being hungry all the time. But it could have been worse. I know we were a lot better off than the Russians and the guys that were captured by the Japanese. Bataan and Corregidor[10]—we heard about what happened there even before we left home. It was in all the newspapers and the newsreels. Anybody who didn't know about that wasn't paying attention to current events.

I felt lucky to be an American. So far as I could tell, the Germans did generally observe the rules of the Geneva Convention for prisoners of war, or at least they did for us.[11] The guards were professionals, just doing their jobs, following orders. I'd say they were pretty businesslike, but most of them could take a joke. We figured it was because the Allies had so many German prisoners by then, maybe they were afraid our side might retaliate against them.

 In May 1942, 10,000 of the 70,000 American and Filipino soldiers captured by the Japanese at Bataan and Corregidor in the Philippines died on the way to prisoner-of-war camps because of deliberate cruelty and neglect, shortage of supplies, or lack of transportation. This has since become known as the Bataan "Death March."

 Germany treated American prisoners of war comparatively well. Although American POWs lost an average of 38 pounds (17 kilograms) in German camps, 99 percent of them survived and eventually were freed. In contrast, American prisoners of the Japanese lost an average of 61 pounds (28 kilograms), and only 73 percent survived. How were German POWs treated in the United States? By all accounts, pretty well. One POW held in Mississippi wrote, "Here we eat more in a single day than during a whole week at home."

UNUSUAL INCIDENTS AT STALAG 17

We were all planning to escape in the spring of 1944. We had a lot of guys in our barracks who were coal miners before the war, so they knew all about digging tunnels. I never actually saw the tunnel they were working on because I wasn't one of the ones who was doing the digging. I mostly just helped guard it, let them know if I thought they were making too much noise or if I saw a guard coming toward them.

The barracks I was in when I first got to Stalag 17 was Number 40, which happened to be the one closest to the main fence that went around the entire camp. Actually, it was two barbed-wire fences about six feet apart, ten feet high. We were only about fifty feet or so from that fence. To the miners, that wasn't very far at all.

I didn't know exactly where the tunnel was, just that it was somewhere between our barracks and the fence. I suspected it was under the wash-trough drain. Nobody but the guys who were doing the actual digging were supposed to know for sure, in case there was a spy among us. One day I heard the tunnel was finished, and we were ready to start using it. Then we saw some guards setting up machine guns out by the fence, so nobody used the tunnel that day.

The day after that, the guards came with a sewer hose and started pumping sewage into the tunnel. They completely flooded our tunnel with sewage. I never heard how the Germans found out about it. There probably was a spy in the barracks, but I don't think anybody ever knew for sure. Even though it was all so secret, it just stands to reason: If you put 250 to 300 guys in one spot, somebody's bound to say something.

If the Germans hadn't discovered the tunnel, I'm not sure if I would have gone through it. Once you got past the fence, there really wasn't anyplace to escape to. Switzerland, I guess. That was the nearest neutral country, but I didn't know how far it was. I knew it was somewhere over the Alps, but even if you got past the mountains you'd probably run into a lot of Germans guarding the border. I don't doubt some of the guys would have tried anyway; I don't know if anybody could have made it.[1]

After the guards flooded the tunnel, they made us move out of our barracks. At first they put us all together in a different building farther away from the fence. Then they started splitting us up. Everybody that used to be in Number 40 got shifted to other barracks—that's when I got separated from my first combine buddy—and pretty soon they tore down the whole building.

That was kind of strange, seeing our old barracks go down. I felt almost sad in a way, but if it hadn't been for that I wouldn't have

 Of the Americans confined to POW camps in Europe, only 737 officers and enlisted men managed to escape and rejoin their own forces.

For religious reasons, many Jews do not eat pork.

German hatred of the Jews was based both on religious and ethnic bias. In addition, many Germans blamed the Jewish community for Germany's economic woes of the 1930s.

met Harold. Harold Kerlanchek was my second combine buddy. We were a lot different from each other; he was a Jewish kid from Brooklyn, which was a big Eastern city, and I was from a small town in the West. He didn't play poker, either, but he'd back me with his cigarettes and then we'd share whatever I won. We both liked the same kinds of food, though, and that's about all any of us ever thought about most of the time. Harold even ate pork.[2]

I don't know why I got along with Harold better than anybody else, but I did. We got to be really good buddies, and that made it a good combine. We both knew about the problems the Jews were having during the war, but it all seemed so far away when we were in the prison camp. Harold did tell me what happened to him in Frankfurt; it sounded like the Nazis interrogated him at the same *Dulagluft* where I was. Harold said they beat him so bad they nearly killed him. He guessed it must have been because of his dog tag. Everybody had his religious preference on his dog tag, so Harold's had a "J" for Jewish.

Anyway, Harold just seemed to accept that this was what Jews should expect. We only talked about it that one time, so I never got a chance to ask him why he felt that way. And I never did understand why the Nazis hated Jews so much.[3] I guess I just always assumed it had something to do with jealousy. I think a lot of the Jews in Germany owned stores and different kinds of businesses, so maybe the Germans were jealous of them because they thought Jews were rich.

I remember there was one other escape attempt at Stalag 17. I'm not too sure about the date, but it had to have been in March or April because it was after the Germans discovered our tunnel. Anyway, it had snowed that night, so these two guys covered themselves up with sheets, thinking they wouldn't be seen as easily. They were creeping along close to the ground and got all the way out to the first fence. They were just chopping through the barbed wire when the prison lights hit them, and then I heard shooting.

I was hiding behind the chimney—the walls of the barracks were so thin I was afraid I'd get hit by the bullets—so I didn't see what was happening. I think one must have been killed right way, or maybe he was just unconscious. The other guy was wounded. We heard him screaming and calling out for help, but there was nothing we could do because it was after dark. If we'd tried to go outside, the guards would have shot us, too. Pretty soon one of the German officers went out and shot them both in the head.

We felt sorry for those guys, but it was their own fault in a way. They knew the risk. They were just desperate, I guess. A lot of guys went crazy like that and got themselves shot one way or another. I remember one guy went completely nuts—took off all his clothes and attacked a guard. I don't know what set him off like that. Maybe he got a letter from home; maybe it was a Dear John. Anyway, they killed him, too. We were pretty mad at that guard for shooting him. He didn't need to do that. He could've just restrained him, but he shot the guy point-blank.

I don't know what kept me from going crazy. My family ties might have had something to do with it. I was getting letters from home and letters from Jackie. Mainly, I think I was just too determined to stay alive in case I ever got a chance to get out.

 D Day (June 6, 1944)—the beginning of Operation Overlord, the Allied invasion of German-occupied Europe. Under the command of U.S. General Dwight D. Eisenhower, Allied forces, including troops, planes, and ships from the United States, Great Britain, Canada, Holland, France, Greece, Norway, and Poland, stormed the beaches at Normandy (France).

Nickname for General Eisenhower.

Sometime in May, I think it was, we heard that Hitler issued a command to kill all the prisoners of war if the war was lost. Then we heard his general staff said no, they wouldn't carry out that command. There were always rumors like that in the prison camp. None of us ever knew which ones to believe.

D Day[4] wasn't a rumor. I knew that was real because guys all over the camp heard about it on their illegal radios. They ran out and spread the word to the rest of us, and pretty soon everybody just started hollering, "Come on, Ike!"[5] That got the attention of the guards; some of them asked us, *"Was ist los?"*—"What is it?" They didn't seem too concerned when we told them.

There wasn't any big celebration or party or anything like that on D Day, probably because we didn't know how much longer the war was going to last. Mostly, we all just stood around that day and felt good. For me, that was the very first time since I'd been shot down that I started to believe I might actually survive.

Sometime after D Day I was in my bunk, asleep. All of a sudden I got woken up. I know it was in the middle of the night, and it had to have been in the summer because all the windows in the barracks were open. There was all this commotion outside, and then I saw the outside lights come on. That was pretty unusual, so it wasn't long before everybody in the barracks was awake. We all wanted to know what was going on, but nobody dared take a step outside. Everybody just crowded around the windows and looked.

I saw guards—there must have been a hundred or more—all of them hurrying from different parts of the camp to go line up in front of the commanding officer. As soon as he had them all standing at attention, he started giving some kind of spiel. Every now and then, he'd stop talking and all the guards would shout "*Heil Hitler!*" Then they'd all click their heels together and salute, and then he'd talk some more. That went on for quite a while, at least an hour, I think.

By then most of us POWs had learned a few German phrases and commands, so we could usually get some idea of what was going on most of the time. We could hear everything the camp commander was saying because he was shouting so loud, but he was talking so fast I couldn't understand the words. All I got was the "*Heil Hitler*" part. It wasn't until the next day that we found out there'd been an attempt to assassinate Hitler by some of his officers.[6] Everything we saw and heard that night must have been part of an exercise to lecture the guards. Maybe it was some kind of a loyalty check, to see if they were still in favor of Hitler. I thought it looked like they were.

Sometime after that—it was still pretty hot weather so it must have been in the summer—I heard that the prisoners in one of the other barracks found a spy. I guess he was a German pretending to be an American. I never heard how they discovered the man was a spy, but I heard he denied it and pleaded for his life. Well, the Americans finally just shoved him outside the barracks after dark. The guards apparently didn't know he was one of their own, so they shot him.

If the guards didn't get you, the camp dogs would. Those dogs were really vicious—German shepherds, of course. They'd bite and attack anybody, and the Germans had them roaming all over the

[6] There were several failed attempts to assassinate Hitler during the war, most of them by his own men. The one that came closest to success was the so-called "General's Plot" on July 20, 1944. (Hitler's injuries were minor.)

camp. I couldn't say how many because we never saw them during the day. The dogs were only let out at night, so the only time you'd see one was if you happened to be looking out a window when it went by the barracks.

We really hated those dogs. We couldn't even go to the latrine at night because of them, so each barracks had a little room with a pit toilet in it. One morning the Germans came in and found a dog in the barracks, dead. I guess somebody killed it and dumped it in the pit toilet.

Another day a bunch of guards came in and told us all to clear out of the barracks. Not just our barracks, every barracks in the American Compound. All four thousand of us had to go outside and stay there for three days and nights. The Germans said it was because they had to search for a certain man they thought was hiding among us, but we didn't believe that was the real reason. Since it happened right after the spy-shooting incident, we all just assumed it was somehow connected to that.

It could have been a way of punishing us for catching their spy. Then again, it might have been nothing more than an excuse for the guards to search the barracks more thoroughly than usual. We wondered if they were looking for something in particular— another tunnel, maybe, or some other big thing their spy might have reported before he got killed. Maybe they just wanted to find all the radios.

Whatever the real reason was, we called it the "big camp out." I remember the weather being pretty warm—July or August, I think—so it wasn't as hard on us as it could have been. They let us take most of our personal belongings, like clothing and blankets, but we weren't allowed to build any fires, so we couldn't cook. Everything just stopped for those three days. Nobody did anything but sit around and talk and wait for the guards to let us back into the barracks.

Toward the end of that first year, we started to notice Allied bombers were flying over our prison camp. We knew we were really deep inside enemy territory, so we figured that meant our side must be winning. Apparently the Germans didn't have many fighter planes left to knock the bombers down, and that got us to teasing the guards. We'd point to the bombers when they went over and say, "*Was ist los?*"—"What is wrong?"—and, "Where's the Luftwaffe?" Most of them would just look up and shrug, but one guard gave me an answer: "*Kein Benzin,*"—"No gasoline"—he said. I didn't know if he knew what he was talking about or not. If he did, I took it to mean the Germans were out of gas.[7]

When Thanksgiving and Christmas came around, there were turkey dinners in cans in our Red Cross parcels. They sent us some instruments, too, so we even had an orchestra and put on a special Christmas program. We didn't have that many illegal radios in the camp at that point, so I didn't get all the war news. I never heard about the Battle of the Bulge[8] until a long time after it was over.

I remember I got a letter from Jackie right around Christmas that year. She said she'd just heard that her cousin Dallas from Iowa had been shot down somewhere over Europe. The family

[7] Due to concentrated Allied bombing of German fuel production facilities during the spring and summer of 1944, the Germans' monthly supply of aviation fuel dropped from 180,000 tons (about 163,000 metric tons) to only 10,000 tons (about 9,000 metric tons) by August. Although there was never a shortage of German fighter planes, there wasn't enough fuel to train new pilots.

[8] Failed but ferocious German offensive against Allies in Ardennes Forest (Belgium and Luxembourg).

knew he was supposed to be alive and captured, but they were still waiting to find out which prison camp he ended up in. Well, I didn't have much else to do, and I knew there were some newer barracks over on the far side of the American Compound. So I went over there and snooped around a little. Sure enough, I found Jackie's cousin. She'd told him all about me, but he was still pretty surprised when I introduced myself. So was Jackie when I wrote back and told her I knew where her cousin Dallas was.

In the spring of 1945 an RAF Pathfinder[9] came over and dropped its flares right about in the middle of our compound. The flares were attached to parachutes. When we saw those things floating down into the camp, we knew we'd just been marked as a target for a bombing raid. About the same time I saw the flares, I heard the air-raid sirens go off.

We were all pretty terrified. We didn't have any air-raid shelters in the prison camp—just some trenches we'd dug—so everybody started running for the trenches. The guards too. Everybody knew a formation of bombers was on the way. The first plane would look for those flares—that's how they knew where they were supposed to drop their bombs—and the rest would drop theirs wherever they saw the first explosions going off. I think that was the scariest thing that happened the whole time I was in prison. I really believed we were going to get bombed and I thought I was going to be killed, or at least injured pretty bad.

It seemed like we stayed in those trenches waiting for the bombers for a long time, but it was actually just a few minutes. I

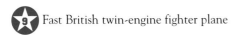
9 Fast British twin-engine fighter plane

1944

COINCIDING DATES

AS THE PRISONERS AT STALAG 17 AWAITED WAR NEWS THROUGHOUT THE SPRING AND SUMMER OF 1944, THE ALLIES STORMED THE BEACHES AT NORMANDY, DEFEATED HITLER IN THE BATTLE OF THE BULGE, AND MADE MORE GAINS IN THE PACIFIC. (SEE TIMELINE.)

Prisoners dug deep trenches in the prison yard as protection from Allied bombing attacks.

don't know what saved us. Maybe somebody in the RAF got smart, maybe some information got through to them at the last second. Somehow, somebody must have realized it was a prisoner-of-war camp they'd marked for a bombing raid. The bombers just passed over us without dropping any of their bombs. I couldn't believe I was still alive.[10]

 The notorious camps at Auschwitz were never bombed either, although American Jewish leaders by this time were well aware of the atrocities carried out there and pleaded with Washington to bomb the crematoriums.

Russian ground forces used T-34 tanks like this one, a powerful weapon, in their advances through German-held territory in Europe in early 1944.

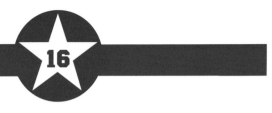

THE MARCH TO GERMANY

On the first of April—I'm sure of that date—the guards told us to prepare to march. All they said was that the Russian army was coming and everybody had to leave the camp before they got there.[1] More than anything, the Germans seemed to be very afraid of capture by the Russians. They didn't say why, but I supposed it was because of the terrible way they'd treated the Russian prisoners of war.[2]

I don't know why the guards didn't just walk away and leave us where we were. They were probably following orders from somebody higher up. They didn't say. They did tell us we could bring anything we wanted to carry, and the rest they were going to burn. I guess that was because of the Russians, too. The Germans probably didn't want to leave anything behind that might help the Russians.[3]

We were all running around, everybody in a hurry, gathering up coats and blankets and whatever food we could lay our hands on.

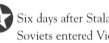 Six days after Stalag 17 was evacuated, the Soviets entered Vienna, approximately 30 miles (48 kilometers) away.

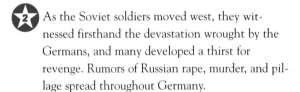 As the Soviet soldiers moved west, they witnessed firsthand the devastation wrought by the Germans, and many developed a thirst for revenge. Rumors of Russian rape, murder, and pillage spread throughout Germany.

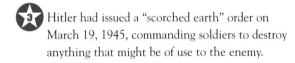 Hitler had issued a "scorched earth" order on March 19, 1945, commanding soldiers to destroy anything that might be of use to the enemy.

Dale Aldrich's Stalag 17 POW dog tag

While we were doing that, the guards were busy hauling stuff out of all the buildings into big piles and lighting fires. Right on top of one pile I saw a pair of GI high-top shoes. They looked like they were brand new. I thought they might fit me, so I grabbed them off the pile. I was kind of disappointed when I saw they were size 6½—I wore a 7—but for some reason I took them anyway. I tied the laces together and hung them around my neck.

I also had this really big box of raisins. I don't remember how I acquired that—probably from a Red Cross parcel—but I remember putting it into a kind of a knapsack I'd made out of cloth, like a hobo. I didn't have much else to bring.

In all the confusion that day, one guy told me he saw a table outside with a bunch of papers on it. I'm sure the Germans were getting ready to burn those too, but he decided to stop and have a look. Somewhere near the top of the pile he recognized my pictures, the ones the Germans took when I first got to Stalag 17. Right next to those he saw my prison dog tag. Since he happened to be a friend of mine, he picked them both out of the pile and gave them to me just as we were leaving the camp. It was the first time I'd seen them. I noticed the German dog tag was different from ours. Instead of two separate pieces of metal, theirs was only one, made so it could be broken in half.

When we left the camp, the Germans divided all the Americans into eight groups of five hundred, and that's how they marched us. They didn't tell us where we were going; we just started south. I don't know how they divided up all the other nationalities that were in the camp. They could have been ahead of us or behind, or maybe the Germans took them off in some other direction alto-gether. I only know that, except for the guards, I never saw anybody but Americans the whole time we were marching.

Schultz was not one of the guards for the group I was in. I don't know what happened to him. He might have been assigned to guard one of the other groups. Whatever it was, I never saw Schultz again. I got separated from Harold that day, too. He wound up in a different marching group with a couple of Jewish guys he knew. Bill Tracy and Tony Svoboda did get put into the same group as me, so I started out walking with them.

The Germans marched us south from Krems until we came to the Danube River. Then they turned us west, and we stayed fairly close to the river the rest of the way. I still didn't know for sure where we were going or how long it would be before we could stop.

We walked all day, every day. While we were on the march, I saw a lot of bombers flying overhead at all different times of the day. It looked like there were hundreds in every formation. I couldn't tell where they were headed, and I didn't see them drop their bombs anywhere near us.[4] I never heard any antiaircraft fire either.

I was awfully hungry during the march; we all were. It was even worse than being in the prison camp, because from the day we left Stalag 17 the Germans didn't make any arrangements for food for the POWs at all. We just had to eat whatever we could find along the way. I saw some kale—it's kind of like cabbage—growing in the fields along the road, so when I ran out of raisins I ate kale. Then I got diarrhea.

POWs on march to Germany

The last major air battle over Europe occurred on April 18, 1945, when 1,211 bombers escorted by 1,200 fighter planes attacked Berlin. Now, with no more targets to destroy, the Allies halted the air campaign against Germany.

One day during the march I was walking along and I saw a farmer planting potatoes. I was so hungry, I stepped off the road and went down into the field and started picking those seed potatoes right out of the dirt. There I was, stealing seed potatoes and stuffing them in my knapsack, when I heard one of the guards yelling at me. *"Nicht! Nicht!"*—"No! No!" he said, and I saw he had his rifle up and pointed at me. He could have shot me, right then and there, but at that particular moment I didn't care if he did or if he didn't. I wanted those potatoes, and I wasn't going to stop until I'd filled my knapsack.

I don't know why that guard didn't shoot me. He probably would have if he'd been one of the Germans. Maybe he was Austrian. Maybe he felt sorry for me. I really don't know. That night when we stopped, I got some water from the river and boiled those potatoes. I ate every one of them, too—didn't share them with anybody.

Nobody shared food during the march. It wasn't anything like when we were in the prison camp. It was just everybody for himself, and it seemed like the only object was to survive if you could on your own. A lot of guys didn't make it. Some got too sick, or else they died from starvation. Whenever somebody fell down and couldn't get up, the rest of us just had to walk around them.

Another day in April—I'm sure of that because we were still in Austria—we were marching through some little town. The guards let us stop for a short rest, and this girl came up to me. She looked to me like she was in her late teens. She didn't speak any English;

she just stood there pointing her finger at my chest and then back at herself. I didn't know what she wanted at first; then I realized it was the shoes. I was so used to having them around my neck since the day I left the prison camp, I'd forgotten they were there. Well, this girl was making it pretty clear she wanted to trade me something for those shoes.

I didn't care about anything but food at that point, so I think I said something like, *"Haben Sie Brot?"*—"Do you have bread?" The girl looked real thoughtful for a couple of seconds, but pretty soon I saw her smile and then she turned around and went running down the street. She must not have had to go very far because she wasn't gone long. And then here she came with a great big loaf of bread. I remember it was round, shaped kind of like a wheel. It was almost as big as she was; I think it must have weighed three or four pounds, at least. The color was light brown—some kind of rye bread, probably. I was so hungry I didn't really notice or care what flavor it was.

When the girl gave me that loaf of bread, I lifted the shoes off my neck and handed them to her. She sat right down on the ground in front of me, pulled off the wooden shoes she had on, and started lacing up those GI high-tops. They must have been a good fit because, boy, was she ever happy. I can still remember how that girl smiled. When the guards told us it was time to get up and march again, I looked back and she was still standing there in her new shoes, smiling and waving at me. I was pretty glad to get that bread, too.

I remember we walked past a lot of farmhouses during the march. One night a couple of guys I knew made a deal with one of the farmers to let us sleep in his barn and buy one of his calves in exchange for cigarettes. We butchered that calf and cooked it the same night. We were so hungry, we just made a big stew and ate as much as we could. After that I went up into the loft to sleep, but then I got diarrhea. I didn't get much sleep that night because I kept having to get up, climb down the ladder, and go outside so many times. I was feeling pretty bad, all right. It wasn't until some time later that I found out it wasn't just diarrhea. It was actually a full-blown case of dysentery.

Three or four days after we butchered and ate the calf, we came to a forest somewhere along the border between Austria and Germany. I don't remember if the guards actually told us that, or if I just assumed it because all of a sudden we just stopped. There was a kind of a clearing in the forest, and that's where we made camp. I don't know what day it was, but I'm positive it was still the month of April. I think we must have walked something like ten miles a day for a little more than two weeks. Altogether, I'd say we marched maybe two hundred miles.

I heard somebody say the nearest town was Braunau [Brno], and somebody else mentioned what a coincidence that was because Braunau happened to be where Hitler was born.[5] I didn't know if that was true or not, and I didn't spend too much time thinking about it.

I thought about Harold, but I was too sick to walk around and look for him. He promised to write to me if he ever made it back

5 Adolf Hitler was born there on April 20, 1889. The town was also known as Braunau am Inn, due to its close proximity to the Inn River, which forms part of Austria's border with Germany.

to Brooklyn, but I never heard from him. I still don't know if he survived. I was pretty sure Bill and Tony were alive because I remembered marching beside them part of the time. I just lost track of them after we stopped and made camp in the forest.

We still didn't have anything to eat, but right then the biggest concern was to get water. There was another river—it was called the Inn River—not too far away from the clear space in the forest. The problem was, you had to climb down this really steep hill to get to it. And then, even if you had a can or something else to carry the water in, you'd spill most of it when you tried to climb back up.

One day when I was down by the water, I got to talking with one of the guards. I'd never seen this one before, but I could tell by the uniform he was an SS trooper. Between his English and my German, I understood him to say he knew the war was just about over, and his side had lost.[6] He also told me he would rather kill himself than be captured. I guess he was afraid of being tortured or some other kind of retaliation, especially by the Russians.

For a German guard, that guy was pretty friendly, and I wouldn't have minded talking to him some more. I even looked for him the next time I went down to the river, but I never saw the man again.

 In late April 1945, American, British, and other Allied armies were driving into Germany from the west while the Soviets advanced from the east. On April 25, the American 69th Infantry met a Russian regiment at the Elbe River in central Germany. Ground superiority had been achieved.

COINCIDING DATES
APRIL 1945 WAS AN IMPORTANT MONTH FOR THE ALLIES. AS ALDRICH AND THE OTHER POWs MARCHED THROUGH AUSTRIA, PRESIDENT ROOSEVELT DIED AND WAS SUCCEEDED BY VICE PRESIDENT HARRY S TRUMAN, U.S. FORCES TOOK THE JAPANESE ISLAND OF OKINAWA, THE ALLIES GAINED CONTROL OF EUROPE, AND ADOLF HITLER, REALIZING THE GAME WAS UP, TOOK HIS OWN LIFE. (SEE TIMELINE.)

1945

LIBERATION

We stayed camped in that forest for a few days, maybe a week. Then, one day—I remember it was May 2—I saw this American officer walking toward us.[1] I didn't see where he came from, but when he got to about the middle of the clearing, he climbed up on a tree stump and said, "You are no longer prisoners of war." That was it. And then he got down off the stump and walked away. He was a captain—ugliest guy I ever saw. He had glasses on and a helmet; there was a pair of .45s on his hips, and he was carrying a rifle. He even had some hand grenades pinned to his shirt. He was downright scary looking.

That night we had a big bonfire to celebrate. Some of the guys went out and found some farmhouses and pretty soon they came back with eggs. Beer, too, in these big, brown quart bottles. I don't know if they traded cigarettes for all the stuff, or whether they just took it. All I know is, after that first night of being liberated, I got *really* sick.

Upon hearing of Germany's unconditional surrender, on May 8, 1945, joyful American civilians and GIs in the United States and overseas celebrated V-E (Victory in Europe) Day.

The next day, two or three jeeps with ten or more American soldiers in each jeep came and captured all our guards. They didn't have to do much capturing because the guards had all given up. I don't know what happened to them; the Americans just marched them away. I remember there was this one old Austrian guard who wanted to go back to his tent first. I'm not sure what it was he wanted to get—I thought I understood him saying something in German about pictures of his family—but the soldiers wouldn't let him. Well, the guard just kept trying to go back to his tent. Finally one of the Americans started beating him, got the old man down on the ground and kicked him with his combat boots until he was unconscious.

I don't want to knock that soldier for what he did. He'd just come from combat on the ground—probably had seen some of his buddies killed. But I felt sorry for that old man. I wanted to help him, but I couldn't. I just didn't feel I should oppose a combat soldier. I was only a gunner. When you're in a war, being in the Air Force is a lot different from being on the ground. It's not that I felt like I was inferior to those guys; it's just that they were *fresh* from combat. And I never actually *saw* any of the people I killed. That makes a difference, too.

We stayed where we were, camped in the forest, for one more day. Some of the guys were still celebrating when another group of American soldiers came. They told us to go to a town that was about five miles away. I don't remember the name of the town; the soldiers just said there was a landing field there and that was where we had to go to get picked up and flown out of Germany. They also said the town had an aluminum factory, which was where we were supposed to stay until the planes came.

Some of the guys I knew had "liberated" a little car. I don't know how they got that either, but they crammed about five guys, including me, inside. Two or three more climbed on top of the car and we rode it that way all the way to the town. There must have been at least eight or ten of us altogether. I don't recall much whooping and hollering during the ride. I know we weren't drunk. I was too sick to drink anything, anyway.

Since we had the car and everybody else had to walk the five miles, of course we were the first ones to make it to the aluminum factory. We snooped around a little bit until we found what must have been the plant manager's office. The first thing we noticed was the plumbing—toilets, sinks, running water. We thought that was pretty nice for a change, so we decided we'd take it over and just camp there. We didn't know how long we were going to have to wait; however long it was, we were planning to spend our time in that office.

As it turned out, we only got to stay for one night because the next day the officers from the liberating army came and claimed it for themselves. We were sure sorry when we had to move out of that office. It felt like a Hilton Hotel after all we'd been through. We ended up having to go downstairs and camp on the main floor of the factory with everybody else. It was a cement floor, but the Army brought in some blankets for us to sleep on. They sent in plenty of food, too, so it wasn't that bad.

Everybody just ate and slept and rested and waited. It took three more days, and finally we heard the planes had come for us. That was the eighth of May.

1945

COINCIDING DATES

WHILE THE POWS WERE BEING LIBERATED, LATE APRIL TO EARLY MAY 1945, GERMANY SURRENDERED ON ALL FRONTS. HOWEVER, PRESIDENT TRUMAN REMINDED AMERICANS THAT THE BATTLE IN THE PACIFIC CONTINUED. (SEE TIMELINE.)

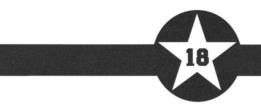

CAMP LUCKY STRIKE

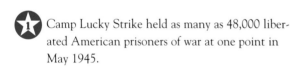
Camp Lucky Strike held as many as 48,000 liberated American prisoners of war at one point in May 1945.

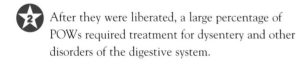
After they were liberated, a large percentage of POWs required treatment for dysentery and other disorders of the digestive system.

From Germany, the planes took us to an air base in France that was close to a town called Nancy [in northeastern France]. We were only there a few hours, and then they put us on a train to Le Havre, which is on the coast of France. Camp Lucky Strike was outside Le Havre. After D Day the Army turned it into a kind of staging area for incoming and outgoing American troops. By the time I got there, Lucky Strike was basically a tent city full of soldiers, mostly POWs, all waiting to go home.[1]

I think I was in the same tent with Bill Tracy. I don't remember much about it because I was so sick, and I guess I was delirious. I'm not sure, but Bill might have been the one that got me to the hospital. The doctor said I was running a fever of 105, and I remember him telling me if it hadn't been for penicillin I probably would have died right there in France.[2]

After five days in the hospital, the doctors still didn't think I was well enough to get out of bed. I was afraid I was going to miss the ship I was assigned to go home on, so I just about cried, begging them to let me out. Finally, one doctor gave in and said he'd sign my release if I promised to keep taking my penicillin.

The reason I was so anxious to get out in time to catch that particular ship was I knew we were traveling by states. Guys from Washington and Oregon and Idaho were all going home together on a certain ship, and guys from other parts of the country got assigned to different ones. If you missed the ship that was carrying the troops from your state, you had to wait until the next one. I was told it might be as long as a month.

If I had it to do over again, I would have stayed in the hospital and missed the ship. It would have given me a month or so in France with nothing to do but travel around and see the sights. I could have gone to Paris and with the war being over in Europe, I could have had a pretty good time. Right then I wasn't thinking that far ahead. All I wanted was to just get back to the States as quick as I could.

After I got out of the hospital, I went back to my tent until it was time to board the ship. I only had about a day and a half to wait, but I remember at some point I felt good enough to get up and walk a little bit. I'd hardly stepped outside the tent when, just by chance, I saw Dick Dabney. I couldn't believe it, but there he was right in front of me. Dabney was the radio-operator gunner for our bomber crew. I thought—we all thought—he'd gone down with the plane. I don't know which of us saw the other first; I think we recognized each other at the same time. I was just so surprised and glad to see him alive.

Dabney told me he and the navigator, Jack Bennett, bailed out of the plane together and landed in some farmer's field. They spent the rest of the afternoon and that whole night hiding in a haystack. It was in December when we got shot down, so Dabney said it was starting to get pretty cold there in that haystack. He remembered the two of them arguing about whether or not they should just give up and come out. The navigator really wanted to, I guess, but Dabney talked him out of it.

Well, according to Dabney, they ended up staying in the haystack all the way to morning. Then the farmer came out and said, "I heard you talking, so I know you're in there. If you want to stay where you are and wait until it gets dark again, I can get the Underground for you."

Well, unlike the guy who found *us*, this one was true to his word. Dabney said the farmer did bring somebody that night, and he and Bennett spent the next six months traveling with the Underground all through Holland and Belgium. I guess they stayed in various houses with different people, all of them connected to the Underground in some way or another, until one night they were at a farmhouse in Belgium and one of their hosts went into town and got drunk. The man apparently got to bragging about how he had a couple of American fliers hiding at his place.

That brought the Belgian Gestapo.[3] Dabney said they came crashing into the house in the middle of the night and caught him

★ **3** The Gestapo, or Nazi State Secret Police, was the most feared branch of the SS.

and Bennett both in bed. They took the man who'd been hiding them outside and shot him. They even killed two women who were also in the house, but for some reason they just took Dabney and Bennett as prisoners of war. Bennett got sent to a prison camp for commissioned officers.

Dabney and I just stood there—we were in something like a street between the tents—talking for quite a while. I was still pretty weak, and he was on his way somewhere. We wished each other luck, and I remember shaking hands with him. We were both anxious to get home. I never saw him again, but I sure was glad to know he made it.

I think it was right around the fifteenth of May when I boarded the ship. It was a lot different from the ship I went overseas on, the *Queen Elizabeth*. There was only enough room for two or three hundred, we were all returning POWs, and everybody was from Washington and Oregon.

This was a real slow-moving cargo boat, one of those Liberty Ships[4] they built real fast because of the war. The Kaiser Corporation built hundreds of them down in California for carrying troops and supplies. Three or four days out of France, the engines quit—not too surprising, considering how hastily those ships were put together. Anyway, there we were, stuck dead in the Atlantic Ocean for two or three days, and then I got seasick.

It was a miserable trip. We had cabins with bunks in them, but there wasn't anything to do except talk and play cards and smoke. We couldn't even smoke out on the deck at night, for fear the light from our matches and cigarettes might attract a sub. Even though

Liberty Ships, part of the merchant fleet, gave American troops and supplies transport to all fronts. Each one could carry 10,900 tons (about 9,900 metric tons) of cargo. By 1945, the Kaiser shipyards in Oregon and California were assembling Liberty Ships from prefabricated parts at the rate of one a day.

the war with Germany was over, we were still fighting the Japanese. We knew it wasn't very likely that a Japanese sub might be in the Atlantic, but it was still possible, so we weren't allowed to show any lights at all after dark.

I think it took us about two weeks altogether to get across the ocean. We finally got to New York somewhere around the end of May.

1945

COINCIDING DATES

WITH THE DEFEAT OF GERMANY IN MAY 1945, THE ALLIES WERE IN A GOOD POSITION TO FOCUS ALL THEIR ATTENTION ON DEFEATING JAPAN. ALREADY THEY OCCUPIED OKINAWA AND IWO JIMA, BUT THE JAPANESE WERE NOT YET READY TO GIVE UP. MEANWHILE ALDRICH AND OTHER POWs WERE RETURNING TO THE UNITED STATES, AND MANHATTAN PROJECT RESEARCHERS PREPARED TO TEST AN ATOMIC BOMB. (SEE TIMELINE.)

HOMECOMING

It was June by the time we got out of New York and back to Camp Kilmer in New Jersey. Since everybody I'd come over with from France was headed for the Northwest, the Army put us all together on the same troop train and sent us to Fort Lewis in Tacoma. That was the same Army base I had to report to when I first got drafted. The base wasn't that much different, but it sure seemed like a lot more than three years since I started my Basic Training there. It felt more like a lifetime.

I only stayed at Fort Lewis for one night, and I had every intention of going to Coulee City the very next day. That was June 18. I even called my mother and told her what time the bus was leaving from Seattle so she'd know when to expect me. While I was standing around the terminal waiting to catch my bus, I ran into Dan Twining. Dan was born and raised in Coulee City, the same as me, so I'd known him and his family all my life. He was working as a janitor at the Greyhound bus terminal. He recognized me right away.

I knew Dan pretty well. He was just a year ahead of me in high school, so we were about the same age. The only reason he didn't get drafted was because he'd been in a car wreck and got crippled. He was living and working there in Seattle during the war, and he wanted me to meet his wife and kids. Nothing would do but for me to come home with him for dinner that night. He just insisted. So finally I gave in and said I would. When I got to his house I had to call my mother again and tell her I was going to be late.

I ended up spending the night at Dan's house. After dinner, we just sat up and talked way into the night. That's when I found out my girlfriend was married. Well, I should say, I was pretty sure. Dan just said he heard there'd been a wedding in her family. I knew it had to have been either her or her sister, and I was pretty positive it was her.

Dan didn't have to go to work in the morning, so I spent the whole next day with him and his family. I was having a good time, but I was anxious to go home. Dan drove me back to the bus terminal, and I caught the first bus I could. I didn't leave Seattle until almost midnight on the nineteenth. There were a lot of other soldiers on the same bus, all getting off and being welcomed along the way. I couldn't see what was going on because it was dark, but I sure could hear the noise every time the bus stopped.

It was about eight o'clock in the morning when the bus finally pulled into Coulee City. The bus stop was on Main Street, right on the corner beside the Chevron gas station. I had hardly slept at all during the trip from Seattle so I was pretty tired, but I remember it was real warm outside when I first stepped off the bus—perfectly normal for a summer morning in Coulee City.

I saw my parents first. We hugged each other, but my mother didn't cry or anything like that. She never showed emotion; she just wasn't that way. My sister Patsy was there, too, and Ted Rice. That was my welcoming committee. I found out my mother had called a whole bunch of people in town and told them when I was coming home, but that was before I told her I was going to stay an extra day in Seattle. I guess quite a few people showed up at the bus stop the day before, but I just wasn't on the bus they were waiting for. Mom said she tried to get the word around that I'd had a change of plans, but apparently a lot more people than she had told heard about my coming home and just came on their own. I thought that was pretty nice, even though I wasn't there to see it.

I don't remember what my mom and dad said when they first saw me. All I remember is wanting to go home. The first thing I did when I got to the house was sit down at the kitchen table. My mother tied on her apron and started cooking me breakfast— bacon and eggs, probably. I think that's what it was.

Sometime after I got home—it might have been that first day—my mother told me my girlfriend got married while I was gone. She married a guy I knew in Coulee City, but I don't want to mention his name, or hers. I guess it happened when I was in the prison camp. Mom said she didn't want me to know about it then. I'd been kind of expecting it, so it wasn't that much of a shock. The only thing that surprised me was hearing it from my mother.

The Army gave me sixty days for R and R so, after I'd been home a while, I decided I'd go to St. Louis and see Jackie. That was in July. In those days, a soldier could take a train and travel anywhere for free. All you had to do was show your serviceman's papers and get on.

Jackie was different than I remembered her. She'd cut her hair and combed it different. I know I didn't like it, but, besides that—well, I don't know what it was exactly. It just seemed like she'd changed a lot.

I stayed in St. Louis at Jackie's house for a couple of days, and then her mother said she wanted all of us to go to Iowa. That was where most of their relatives lived, including the aunts I'd already met when they were at Jackie's house for Christmas back when I was in Air College. So Jackie's whole family and I piled into her car and drove to Iowa. Eldora was the name of the town.

Eldora wasn't a very big place. Bigger than Coulee City, but that's not saying much. Jackie's family had a reunion after we got there, and she introduced me to all her cousins. Of course, I'd already met Dallas. He and his girlfriend went roller-skating one night with Jackie and me. Another time, we went shopping and I bought Jackie a ring. It was a pretty good-sized diamond—I paid three hundred dollars for it—but I never actually proposed to her.

Jackie truly expected we were going to get married. I don't think I was ever that sure, even when I gave her the ring. I guess I just wanted to make her happy. I know I was grateful to her for being so faithful, and for all the letters I got from her when I was in the prison camp. Those letters really helped.

I think I always knew things weren't going to work out the way Jackie had it all planned. For one thing, she made it real clear she was never going to live anywhere but St. Louis. She couldn't go away and leave "Mama." Well, I knew I didn't want to live in St. Louis, so that was a big part of it. The rest, I don't know, except to say it just wasn't there. It was for her, but not for me. I just wasn't quite ready to tell her.

Between St. Louis and back and forth to Iowa, I was with Jackie for about two weeks altogether. She wanted to come back to Coulee City with me and meet my family. I said no because I was still in the service and the Army wanted me in California pretty soon. Well, then she wanted me to take her with me down to California. I said no to that, too. Even though I could travel for free, I'd have had to pay for her. After spending all that money on her ring, I didn't think I could afford it. All that was true, but it wasn't the whole truth. By that time I was pretty close to a hundred percent certain I wasn't going to marry her. For some reason, I just couldn't seem to say it out loud.

My original orders were to report to the base in Santa Monica, California, at the end of August, but the war ended about that time so the Army extended my R and R for another thirty days. I spent most of that extra time—the nights, anyway—in Grand Coulee. With all the workers there because of the [Grand Coulee] dam,[1] there were lots of taverns and bars where you could go to dance. That's where I met Lila McKinney. Lila had a job in one of the warehouses. She lived in this women's dormitory where they got their meals and maid service and everything. I guess the govern-

 A huge gravity dam constructed between 1933 and 1942 to generate electricity and provide water for irrigation.

ment built several of those places for the single men and women who worked on the dam.

Lila liked to go out dancing at night. She told me she even entered one of those jitterbug[2] contests they used to have at the USO during the war. The prize was only a carton of Lucky Strike cigarettes—and she didn't smoke—but, anyway, she won.

So, one night Lila and I were out dancing to piano music in this Grand Coulee tavern called the Wig Wam, when Ted Rice and his wife, Mary, came in. The four of us sat down across from each other in a booth, and I mentioned I had to go to Santa Monica. Ted said, "Why don't we all drive down to Santa Monica together? You and Lila and Mary and me."

We figured it would take us about three days to get there, but with the war over we didn't have to worry about gas rationing anymore. Lila said she'd never been to California before, and it sounded like fun. She even had some time off coming, so she could go if she wanted to. We hadn't known each other for very long, but she liked me pretty well, and she must have figured I was a gentleman. We ordered another round of drinks and started talking about driving to Santa Monica in my car.

I was pretty proud of that car. It was a 1934 Ford two-door. Brand new, it would have cost over a thousand dollars, but I'd bought it, used, before the war for only two hundred dollars. I didn't have a bit of trouble with it either, all the way down to California and back. The only thing that happened was I got a flat tire, but that wasn't until right when we got home. I couldn't believe that.

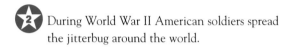

During World War II American soldiers spread the jitterbug around the world.

On the road we stayed in motels—Mary and Lila in one room and Ted and me in another, except for one night when we couldn't find a vacancy. Then we all slept in the car. When we got to Santa Monica, Ted and Mary went to stay with some relatives, Lila got a hotel room, and I went to the Army base. I was sent there to get a medical checkup, which was all right, but then the doctor said the Army lost my records and I'd have to get another typhoid shot. I tried to talk him out of it, or at least put it off a day because Lila and I had plans to go to a dance on the base that night. The doctors were all real sympathetic, but I still got the typhoid shot.

Well, of course I knew that shot was going to make me sick, so I went out and bought myself a bottle of whiskey. I guess I figured if I drank some of that I wouldn't feel the effects of the shot so much. That was a mistake. By the time I got to the hotel to pick up Lila, I was a mess—stumbling around, vomiting in the elevator, and the whole bit. When I finally found Lila's room, I guess I tried to get a little too affectionate. She threw me out, of course, and neither of us went to the dance. I apologized and explained it all to her the next day, but, except for the drive back home, we didn't see too much of each other after that.

I stayed at the base in Santa Monica for about a week. After all my medical tests and checkups were done with, the Army gave me a choice. I could ask for reassignment to a new unit, or, since the war was over, I could get out. The Army had this point system.[3] You got a certain number of points for your time in the military and for the kind of duty you served. I had enough points to get out. I thought about staying in for about two seconds. I was tired of it.

 Under the point system, men with the most points were rotated home first. Those with the fewest points were assigned occupation duty in Germany.

Dale Aldrich on November 19, 1945, at Fort George Wright, Spokane, Washington. "I would have shaved if I'd known they were going to take my picture that day," he said.

The Army sent me to Fort George Wright in Spokane in October. All I had to do was wait for them to process my discharge papers, so I took a bunch of R-and-R-type classes—golf, radios, and stuff like that—just to pass the time. I got promoted to staff sergeant while I was there. That was the promotion I was scheduled for when I was in England, but I got shot down before it came through. I didn't get the higher rank and pay until after I was home.

I got my formal discharge on November 19, 1945. That was really dumb of me. I could have—should have—stayed in the service until spring. It would have been easier for me to find a civilian job if I'd waited another six months or so. I guess I didn't think about that at the time.

I just wanted out. I wanted to start my life again.

1945

COINCIDING DATES

IN AUGUST 1945, WHILE DALE ALDRICH AWAITED DISCHARGE FROM THE AIR FORCE, PRESIDENT TRUMAN—HOPING TO END THE WAR IN ONE DECISIVE ACTION—ORDERED THE AIR FORCE TO DROP AN ATOMIC BOMB ON HIROSHIMA, JAPAN. ALTHOUGH MORE THAN 100,000 PEOPLE WERE KILLED OR INJURED, THE JAPANESE DID NOT SURRENDER. ON AUGUST 9, THE UNITED STATES DROPPED ANOTHER ATOMIC BOMB—THIS TIME ON NAGASAKI. FINALLY, ON AUGUST 10, A MESSAGE OF SURRENDER ARRIVED. WORLD WAR II WAS FINALLY OVER. (SEE TIMELINE.)

DALE WILFRED ALDRICH

I was born February 23, 1921, in Coulee City, Washington. My parents were Clifford Heath—everybody called him C.H.—and Beatrice Pearl Aldrich. My dad was German; my mother was English. Her maiden name was Plunkett. They moved to Coulee City in 1920, the summer before I was born.

I had two older brothers. C.H. Jr. was the oldest. He died from a brain tumor when he was in high school. I was in the seventh grade when that happened. He and I had grown up together, so it hit me pretty hard. My other brother was Neil. He died when he was about two years old, before I was born. Mom wasn't quite sure what made him so sick. She thought he'd eaten too many green apples. Whatever it was, I guess he just got so dehydrated that he died. There wasn't much medical help for that in those days.

Donna and Polly were my two older sisters. Polly died in May of 1997. I also have my sister Patsy Joy. She's the only one in the family younger than I am.

My dad owned Aldrich Motors in Coulee City. It was a car sales and service business right there on Main Street. Starting with the old Model Ts, Dad sold Fords from 1927 until he retired and sold the business to Perry Brown in 1957.

I graduated from Coulee City High School in June of 1939. That summer I went to work as a laborer for the Bonneville Power Administration. All those power lines you see in the Grand Coulee area—I helped do the surveys for those. I got paid a dollar an hour for that, which was considered pretty good money at the time.

In the fall of 1939, I started college at WSU [Washington State University, Pullman, Washington]. I was majoring in business administration, but college was expensive, so after the first year I went back to work for Bonneville until the fall of 1941. I could only afford one more semester before I had to quit school again in the spring of 1942. That's when I started driving tractor for Chris Ottmar, one of the farmers in Coulee City. I was living with my parents and planning to save all summer so I could go back to WSU in the fall.

Altogether, I only got to go to college for a year and a half before I was drafted. I was starting to lean toward changing my major to electrical engineering. If I'd done that, I might not have been drafted. As it was, I was still in business administration. Business majors didn't get student deferments.

I don't know how my life would have turned out differently if I hadn't gone to war. For sure, I would have finished college. I know I could have gone back to school on the GI Bill[1] after the war was over, but somehow I never did. I just started looking for a job as

Popular name for the Servicemen's Readjustment Act of 1944, which appropriated federal money to help veterans pay for college, buy housing, and start businesses.

soon as I got out of the service until I finally got on at the Union Oil distribution plant in Coulee City in the spring of '46. Between that and starting my own family, I guess I just got too busy to think about college.

I think I knew all along I wasn't going to marry Jackie. I finally ended up writing her a letter in the spring of 1946. Shortly after that, one of Jackie's girlfriends wrote to my mother and said Jackie was having a nervous breakdown because of that letter. I felt bad, but there wasn't anything else to say. I never saw Jackie again.

Later that same spring, some friends of mine wanted me to drive them to a movie in Grand Coulee. I said I would if they'd get a girl for me, so they called this girl they knew who was in town for a visit. Her name was Wanda Lea.

Even though it was just a blind date, Wanda and I really hit it off. We got married on the fifth of July, 1946. I have four children from that marriage: Steven was born in 1947; Janie in 1949; Stanley in 1953; Timothy in 1960. And, as of now [1999], I have ten grandchildren and three great-grandchildren.

About fifteen years after I was married, Jackie's mother wrote to me. She wanted me to know Jackie had got married and was real happy, living on a farm in Iowa with her husband and children. In the same envelope with the letter, all wrapped up in a piece of tissue, there was the diamond ring I'd given her in the summer of 1945. I took it to a jeweler and had the stone put into a different setting for my wife. She really liked that ring and wore it all the time.

Several years after I got home, a stranger came into the tavern in Coulee City. I was standing behind the bar, helping the bartender. The man looked straight at me and said, "Where were you on December 22, 1943?" I said, "Bailing out of a plane, same as you." It was Jack Bennett, the navigator. I hadn't seen him since the day we were shot down, but I recognized him as soon as he came in.

Jack and I talked for quite a while about what happened. He said he was probably the last one to see our pilot and copilot alive. Just before he bailed out, Jack said he looked in the cockpit and saw Lembcke trying to help Mangis put on his parachute harness. The rest of us kept our harnesses on all the time we were in the air, but Mangis never did. He always said it was too bulky and uncomfortable to wear in the cockpit.

Another thing that happened a few years after I got home. A movie came out called *Stalag 17*.[2] That got my attention because it was the name of the prison camp I was in for a year and a half. The movie was supposed to be based on the reports of some prisoners who'd been there, and William Holden was the star. When it finally came to the theater in Grand Coulee I asked my dad if he wanted to go and see it with me. I'd say it was pretty realistic, for a movie—more than any of the others I've seen. Especially the part about the German spy in the barracks; how he was discovered by the Americans and killed by the guards. I was there when that happened, and I remember all of us speculating that was why the Germans made us move out of the barracks for three days.

Some parts of that movie were kind of painful to watch, but after my dad and I saw it together I started talking to him more. I told him about my experiences with the bomber crew, what it was

A 1953 film directed by Billy Wilder.

like to be a prisoner of war. Dad was very interested. I suppose he was proud of me for surviving. He never had any war experience himself, but he talked to me about his youth—mainly about how hard he had to work as a laborer when he was still in high school.

I have four medals. The Purple Heart is for being wounded. I wish I could find that one, but I don't know where it is anymore. I also have the World War II Victory Medal—everybody got one of those—the Good Conduct Medal, and the POW Medal for being a prisoner of war. [Aldrich later realized he had also misplaced his Good Conduct Medal.]

I belong to an organization called American Ex-Prisoners of War. I usually go to the meetings in Spokane on the second Friday of every month, except for when the roads get bad in the winter. That's where I met Sam Grashio. Sam was a second lieutenant during the war, captured by the Japanese. He told me if somebody tried to escape from them, they would just select ten guys alphabetically and shoot them as a deterrent to the rest. He said he felt guilty after he escaped, knowing there were probably ten guys killed because of him. He wrote a book called *Escape to Freedom*. You can get it at the PX at Fairchild Air Force Base in Spokane.

Wanda and I were divorced in 1984. In May of that same year, Ted and Mary Rice told me they'd seen Lila at the country club. She told them her husband had died, and she was living in Ephrata. That was only about thirty miles from Coulee City, and I was feeling pretty lonesome about then. So, forty-one years after she got so mad at me in that hotel room in Santa Monica, I called Lila on the phone and asked her if she'd give me another chance—

Purple Heart with Bronze Oak Leaf Cluster   **Victory Medal**   **Good Conduct Medal**

Prisoner of War Medal   **Europe-African-Middle Eastern Campaign Medal with Silver Service Star**   **American Campaign Medal**

Aldrich's two lost medals, first awarded in 1945, were reissued to him in November 1999. Further review of Aldrich's military record resulted in the awarding of two additional medals in November 1999.

Dale Aldrich returned to Austria in 1996 to visit the site of Stalag 17. A single monument marks the spot. Roughly translated, the inscription reads: "During the time of the Second World War, the prisoner-of-war camp Stalag 17B was located in this vicinity. Those captives who died are buried in the Krems City Cemetery, or [their remains] were sent to their home areas."

if she'd have dinner and dance with me again. She said yes, and it was just like old times. Pretty soon it got to be a joke around town about how I was wearing tracks in the road between Coulee City and Ephrata from all my driving back and forth to see Lila.

It took us about two years to decide we were reacquainted enough to get married. The wedding was at her daughter's house on Mercer Island [a suburb of Seattle] on April 27, 1986.

Lila and I have done quite a bit of traveling together. In 1996 we took a trip to Austria with a whole group of ex-prisoners of war. We walked all over the ground where Stalag 17 used to be, but all the buildings are gone. The fences, too. The only way you'd know it used to be a POW camp is if you can find this plaque on a stone with a cross on it. I don't know who put it there—the writing's in German—but that's all there is in the middle of a meadow, about thirty miles outside Vienna.

While I was in Austria, I asked some of the guys I was with if they remembered this or that place, or some of the things that happened when we were prisoners. They said they didn't. I don't know if they really can't recall any of it, or if it's because they don't want to. Some things I don't remember either, but there's still a lot I'd just as soon forget, if I could.

About fifty years after I was shot down—I think it was in 1992 or 1993—I got a letter from Mangis Jr. He couldn't have been more than two or three when his dad was killed, but he was the oldest of Mangis's two children. He said he was living in Salem, Oregon, and that he worked for the state. He wanted to know what I could tell him about his dad, so I wrote back and told him what hap-

The heavily armed B-17s were known as Flying Fortresses. Here visitors at Geiger Field, Spokane, Washington, view the "Nine-O-Nine," a restored B-17G.

The author gets an up-close view of the ball turret of a restored B-17G.

pened the day we were shot down. Then he wrote me again and asked if I could tell him any stories about his father. There wasn't too much I could tell him, because I never had that much to do with the pilot. None of the gunners did. I thought about telling him how his dad flunked that first instrument test in St. Louis because he'd been out partying all night, but then I decided maybe I shouldn't tell him that.

I've been thinking about Mangis a lot lately. I think the reason he decided not to head for Sweden after we had to drop out of our formation was because he didn't want anybody to accuse him of being a coward. And I think when he realized we weren't going to make it back to England after all, he might have been trying to hold the plane steady to give the crew the best chance to bail out. He just held it a little too long, and that's why he didn't get himself out in time. Mangis was anything but a coward. It's very possible he gave his life to save the rest of us.

I still have nightmares about the day I was shot down. I don't get them as often as I used to—less than once a month, maybe two or three times a year. The nightmares are always the same. It's just a replay of those last few minutes before I bailed out of the plane. I wake up screaming and hollering real loud, and I feel really cold.

After I'm awake, if I can get myself warm, I can usually go back to sleep. Sometimes I can't. I just have to stay awake and think about it.

MEMORIES OF DADDY

I must have been a very small child, perhaps three or four years of age, when my very handsome, smiling daddy lifted me, light as a feather, onto his lap and shared his heart with me.

I remember holding a large book in my chubby hands; the book contained pictures of airplanes and other handsome, smiling daddies. My daddy told me they were his friends, his war buddies, and he shared the story of how he was "shot down" over Germany, imprisoned, and finally marched to freedom. In my child's mind I imagined him "falling" into hell, conquering the "enemy," and marching out victorious.

I remember fingering the war medals—my favorite was the Purple Heart—and feeling an outpouring of love for him. What he had done was beyond my ability to speak, but my daddy taught me what courage meant at an early age through his storytelling.

As I grew older, there were no more talks of war, and the books were closed and put away. However, the imprinting in my mind remained to grow ever brighter and more vivid, and the memories are alive in me yet today.

Indeed, the veterans of World War II were every bit as gallant and courageous as I imagined. Collectively these good men changed the shape and substance of our world, gave hope to the hopeless, freedom to the oppressed, inspiration to the youth, and confirmation of life to us all.

Janie Aldrich Hickel

GLOSSARY

basic training: the first phase of military training.

bedbug: a tiny, wingless bloodsucking insect that infests houses, particularly beds, and preys on humans and other mammals. It is known to carry dangerous diseases.

buck private: a private is an enlisted person of low rank; a buck private is the lowest grade of private.

Class A uniform: standard Army uniform.

commissioned officer: one who has been appointed to a U.S. military rank of at least O-1, which is 2nd Lieutenant in the Army, Air Force, or Marines.

concentration camp: a camp or prison compound where prisoners of war, political prisoners, or refugees are detained or confined.

contrails: white streaks of condensed water vapor that form behind high-flying aircraft; also known as vapor trails.

Dear John: a letter in which a girlfriend breaks off an engagement or relationship or a wife asks for a divorce.

debriefing: an interrogation or questioning conducted after a military operation.

deferred: temporarily excused from military service.

drafted: required to serve in a nation's armed forces.

dysentery: a disease of the large intestine easily spread by food or drink contaminated by shigella bacteria.

emphysema: a respiratory disease characterized by coughing, shortness of breath, and wheezing; can develop into extreme difficulty in breathing and even disability or death. Common among heavy cigarette smokers.

formation: a large number of bombers flying very close together for mutual protection from enemy fire.

gassed: poisoned or attacked with chemical weapons such as chlorine and mustard gases.

hope chest: a box or chest used by young women to hold clothing and household furnishing such as linens in anticipation of marriage.

jitterbug: an American dance for couples popular in the 1930s and 40s; descended from the similar lindy hop.

mess hall: a hall or building in which mess (food) is served.

morphine: a pain-killing narcotic derived from opium.

newsreel: a short motion picture showing current events.

noncommissioned officer: a sergeant or other subordinate officer appointed from among enlisted men.

R and R: rest and recreation, or rest and recuperation.

scorched-earth policy: military practice of destroying anything that might be of use to the enemy, including crops and livestock.

sergeant: a noncommissioned officer of the Army, Air Force, or Marines.

FOR FURTHER READING

Adler, David A. *We Remember the Holocaust*. New York: Holt, 1989.

Armstrong, O.K. *The Fifteen Decisive Battles of the United States*. New York: David McKay, 1961.

Bailey, Ronald H. *Prisoners of War*. Alexandria, VA: Time-Life Books, 1981.

Bird, Tom. *American POWs of World War II: Forgotten Men Tell Their Stories*. Westport, CT: Praeger, 1992.

Black, Wallace B., and Jean F. Blashfield. *Bataan and Corregidor*. New York: Crestwood House, 1991.

Bowers, Peter M. *50th Anniversary Boeing B-17 Flying Fortress: 1935–1985*. Seattle: Museum of Flight, 1985.

Bowman, Martin W. *Thunder in the Heavens: Classic American Aircraft of World War II*. New York: Smithmark, 1994.

Boyne, Walter J. *Silver Wings: A History of the United States Air Force*. New York: Simon and Schuster, 1993.

Bullock, Alan. *Hitler: A Study in Tyranny*. New York: Harper and Brothers, 1952.

Byers, Ann. *The Holocaust Camps*. Springfield, NJ: Enslow, 1998.

Campbell, John, ed. *The Experience of World War II*. New York: Oxford University Press, 1989.

Craven, Wesley and James Lea Cate, eds. *The Army Air Forces in World War II*. Volume Six. Seven Volumes. Washington D.C.: Office of Air Force History, 1983.

Crosby, Harry H. *A Wing and a Prayer: The "Bloody 100th" Bomb Group of the U.S. Eighth Air Force in Action Over Europe in World War II*. New York: Harper Collins, 1993.

Cross, Robin. *The Bombers*. New York: Macmillan, 1987.

Dank, Milton. *D-Day (Turning Points of World War II)*. New York: Watts, 1984.

Davis, Larry. *B-17 in Action*. Carrollton, TX: Squadron/Signal, 1984.

Dear, I. C. B., ed. *The Oxford Companion to World War II*. Oxford: Oxford University Press, 1995.

Dupuy, Trevor Nevett. *The Air War in the West: June 1941–April 1945*. In *The Military History of World War II*, 18 vols. New York: Watts, 1963.

Durand, Arthur R. *Stalag Luft III*. Baton Rouge: Louisiana State University Press, 1988.

Ethell, Jeff. *B-17 Flying Fortress*. Osceola, WI: Motorbooks, 1995.

Fletcher, Eugene. *The Lucky Bastard Club: A B-17 Pilot in Training and in Combat, 1943–45*. Seattle: University of Washington Press, 1992.

Frank, Anne. *The Diary of a Young Girl*, trans. B. M. Mooyaart-Doubleday. New York: Doubleday, 1952.

Freeman, Roger A. *Target Germany*. Volume 4, in *Making War in the Twentieth Century*. London: Marshall Cavendish, n.d.

Gansberg, Judith M. *Stalag U.S.A.: The Remarkable Story of German POWs in America*. New York: Crowell, 1977.

Gilbert, Martin. *The Second World War: A Complete History*. New York: Holt, 1989.

Gunston, Bill. *Combat Aircraft of World War II*. New York: Bookthrift, 1978.

Hurd, Charles. *The Compact History of the American Red Cross*. New York: Hawthorn Books, 1959.

Krull, Kathleen. *V is for Victory*. New York: Knopf, 1995.

Leckie, Robert. *The Story of World War II*. New York: Random House, 1964.

Lingeman, Richard R. *Don't You Know There's a War On?: The American Home Front, 1941–1945*. New York: G.P. Putnam's Sons, 1970.

Mason, Herbert Molloy, Jr. *Duel for the Sky: Fighter Planes and Fighting Pilots of World War II*. New York: Grosset and Dunlap, 1970.

McCullough, David G. *The American Heritage World War II Chronology*. New York: American Heritage, 1966.

Parrish, Thomas, ed. *The Simon and Schuster Encyclopedia of World War II*. New York: Simon and Schuster, 1978.

Perret, Geoffrey. *Winged Victory: The Army Air Forces in World War II*. New York: Random House, 1993.

Potter, Lou. *Liberators: Fighting on Two Fronts in World War II*. New York: Harcourt Brace, 1992.

Pyle, Ernie. *Brave Men*. New York: Holt, 1944.

Reeder, [Colonel] Red. *The Story of the Second World War*. New York: Hawthorn Books, 1970.

Ryan, Cornelius. *The Longest Day: June 6, 1944*. New York: Simon and Schuster, 1959.

Scherman, David E., ed. *Life Goes to War*. New York: Little Brown, 1977.

Sears, Stephen W. *Air War Against Hitler's Germany*. New York: American Heritage, 1964.

Steins, Richard. *The Allies Against the Axis: World War II (1940–1950)*. New York: Twenty-First Century Books, 1993.

Thomas, Dianne Stine, ed. *World War II: Time-Life Books History of the Second World War*. New York: Prentice-Hall, 1989.

Toland, John. *The Last 100 Days*. New York: Random House, 1965.

World War II: A Fiftieth Anniversary History by the Writers and Photographers of the Associated Press. New York: Holt, 1989.

Wright, Michael, ed. *The World at Arms: The Reader's Digest Illustrated Story of World War II*. Pleasantville, NY: The Reader's Digest Association, 1969.

INDEX

Page numbers in *italics* refer to illustrations.

Air College, 15–18, 21
Aircraft recognition training, 26
Aldrich, Beatrice Pearl, 11, 36,
   95, 133, 139
Aldrich, C.H. Jr., 139
Aldrich, Clifford Heath, 36, 133,
   139, 140, 142–143
Aldrich, Donna, 139
Aldrich, Lila McKinney,
   135–137, 143, 145
Aldrich, Neil, 139
Aldrich, Patsy Joy, 47, 133, 139
Aldrich, Polly, 139
Aldrich, Stanley, 141
Aldrich, Steven, 141

Aldrich, Timothy, 141
Aldrich, Wanda Lea, 141, 143
American Ex-Prisoners of War,
   143
Army Air Corps, 13
Auschwitz concentration camp,
   84, 85, 113
"Autumn crisis" of 1943, 39
Aviation fuel, 111

B-17 bombers (Flying Fortresses),
   146
   ball turret of, 34, 35, *35, 146*
   bomb bay of, 31, *33*
   bombing missions, 47–49, *50,*
      51–52, 54–55, 57–63
   cockpit of, *29*
   crew of, 28–29, *30*

B-17 bombers (*cont.*)
   diagram of, *32*
   flight suits, 35–36
   guns on, 31, 34, 48
   Princess Pat, 47–48
      radio room of, 31, *33*
      speed of, 64
      training flights, 35, 37–38
Basic Training, 14–15
Bataan "Death March," 103
BBC (British Broadcasting
   Company), 99
Bedbugs, 97
Bennett, Jack, 30, 40, 73,
   128–129, 142
Beobachter, 97
Berlin, Germany, 55, 57, 117
Biggs, Bob, 11
Braunau (Brno), 120
British prisoners, 86, 91
Bulge, Battle of the, 111

Camp Kilmer, 41, 42, 131
Camp Lucky Strike, 126–128
Cannons, 66
Celusnak, L.J., 29, 30, 40, 72–75
Chemical weapons, 20
Cologne, Germany, 77
"Combat box" formation, 51
Concentration camps, 84
Corregidor, 103

D Day, 108
Dabney, Dick, *30*, 31, 65–66, 73,
   127–129
Danube River, 117
DiMaggio, Joe, 99
Dog tags, 13, *116*, 116
Draft, 11–12
Drop tanks, 61
Dulagluft, 79–82, 106

Eisenhower, Dwight D., 108
Elbe River, 121
Emden, Germany, 51
Escape to Freedom (Grashio), 143

Faragasso, F., 29, *30*, 76
Flight jackets, 40, *41*
Flight suits, 35–36
Fort George Wright, 138
Frankfurt, Germany, 76, 77
French prisoners, 86, 95

"General's Plot" of 1944, 109
Geneva Convention Relative to
   the Treatment of Prisoners
   (1929), 26, 73, 75, 77, 85, 93,
   103
German prisoners, 103
Gestapo, 128–129
GI Bill, 140
Grand Coulee Dam, 135

Grashio, Sam, 143
Gunnery school, 25–26

Hickel, Janie Aldrich, 141,
    148
Himmler, Heinrich, 93
Hitler, Adolf, 9, 12, 81, 84, 108,
    109, 115, 120
Hogan's Heroes (television show),
    101
Holden, William, 142
Holland, 69–71, 128
Holocaust, 84, 85, 94
Horham Air Base, 45–48

IFF (Identification, Friend or Foe)
    device, 62
Inn River, 120, 121
Italian prisoners, 86, 95

Jefferson Barracks, Missouri, 15
Jews, 84, 85, 106
Jitterbug contests, 136
Jorgensen, Ralph, 56
Ju-88 fighter plane (Junkers), 26,
    64, *64*, 65

Kaiser Corporation, 129
Kerlanchek, Harold, 106, 117,
    120–121
Krema, Austria, 84, 117

Lembcke, D.F., 29, 30, 36, 73,
    142
Liberty Ships, 129
Lice, 85, 97
Lowry Field, 34
Luftwaffe, 52, 66

"Mae West" life jacket, 65, *65*
Mangis, M.W., 28, *30*, 36, 38–41,
    47, 51, 52, 62, 63, 65, 73, 145,
    147
Martin gunner, 31
McMaster, Bill, *30*, 33–34, 39,
    66–68, 70, 73
Medals, *143*, 143, 148
Me-109G fighter plane, 65, *65*
Mengele, Josef, 85
Messerschmitts, 26, 64, 65
Moses Lake, Washington, 27, 28,
    36
Münster mission, 57–63

Nazi party, 12
95th Bomber Group, 46
Norden bombsight, 29

Officer Candidate School (OCS),
    29, 31
Oxygen masks, 64
P-38 Lightning fighter plane, 26,
    61

P-47 Thunderbolt fighter plane, 26, 61, 83
P-51 Mustang fighter plane, 62
Parcel Day, 90, 91–93
Parks Air College, 16–18, 21
Pathfinder fighter plane, 112
Pearl Harbor, 8, *10*, 11
Penicillin, 126, 127
Point system, 137

Queen Elizabeth (liner), 42, *43*, 44

Radar, 44, 59
Red Cross, 20, 77, 91–97, 99, 111
Regensburg, Germany, 39, 55
Rice, Mary, 136–137, 143
Rice, Ted, 36–37, 98, 133, 136–137, 143
Russian prisoners, 93–94, 103, 115

San Antonio Air Base, 22–24
Schultz, Corporal, 101–103, 117
Schweinfurt, Germany, 39, 55
"Scorched earth" order, 115
Short, Jack, *30*, 34, 35, 58, 66–68, 70, 73
69th Infantry, 121
Spokesman Review, The, 81–82
SS (*Schutzstaffel*), 81
Stalag 17, 84–86, *87*, 88–89, 90, 91–114, *97*, *113*, *144*, 145

Stalag 17 (movie), 142
Strafing runs, 83
Submarines, 44
Svoboda, Tony, *30*, 34, 68–70, 72–74, 76, 79, 82, 85, 91, 117, 121

T-34 tank, *114*
335th Squadron, 46
Tokyo tanks, 63
Tracy, Bill, *30*, 31, 65, 70, 72–74, 76, 79, 82, 85, 91, 117, 121, 126
Twining, Dan, 131–132

Underground, 70, 72, 128
U.S. Eighth Air Force, 46
USO (United Service Organizations), 18, *19*, 20

V-E (Victory in Europe) Day, *123*
Vienna, Austria, 115

Walla Walla, Washington, 37, 38
Williams, Ted, 99
World War I, 20

Yugoslav prisoners, 86

Zero fighter planes, 26

PHOTO CREDITS

1944

6 D Day. Allied troops storm Normandy beaches; beginning of Operation Overlord to liberate Europe from German occupation.

22 USSR launches attack on Germany from east.

JULY
20 Plot by high-ranking Germans to assassinate Hitler fails.

AUGUST
25 Allies liberate Paris after four years of Nazi occupation.

OCTOBER
21 Japanese begin kamikaze attacks on Allied warships in Pacific.

23–26 Battle of Leyte Gulf, largest naval battle in history. Japanese fail to block U.S. landings in Philippines.

30 Last use of gas chambers at Auschwitz.

NOVEMBER
24 First major Allied daylight bombing mission of Japan.

25 At Auschwitz Germans try to erase evidence of Nazi genocide; crews scrape human fat from chimneys where bodies were burned.

27 American bombers begin renewed attack on Germany. Despite massive defensive action, German losses are nearly 10 to 1.

DECEMBER
16 Battle of the Bulge begins; Hitler wages last major offensive of war against Allied forces in Ardennes Forest (Belgium and Luxembourg).

24 Largest single bombing strike of war: 2,034 American bombers attack German forces in Ardennes.

1945

JANUARY
12 Largest offensive of war: Soviets advance toward Germany through eastern Europe.

16 Allies defeat German forces at Battle of the Bulge; Germans retreat eastward.

FEBRUARY
4-11 Yalta Conference. Roosevelt, Churchill, Stalin meet; discuss war strategy and how to divide Germany at war's end.

19 (- March 26) U.S. Marines capture Iwo Jima, island in Pacific, but suffer highest casualty rate in Marine history.

MARCH
7 Americans take Cologne, then seize bridge across the Rhine so Allies can cross into central Germany.

9-10 Massive American firebombing attack on Tokyo.

15 Anne Frank and her sister die of typhus in German concentration camp.